The Reminiscences
of
Admiral Alfred M. Pride
U.S. Navy (Retired)

U.S. Naval Institute
Annapolis, Maryland
1984

Preface

Naval history is indeed enhanced by having available the following recollections of Admiral Pride, for he played a pioneering role in many facets of naval aviation from the early 1920s onward. He was, for instance, in the first crew of the first U.S. aircraft carrier, the Langley, and had a substantial role in the development of flight deck arresting gear for that ship and two subsequent carriers, Lexington and Saratoga. Pride was the first man to take off and land a plane on the Lexington. He had several tours of duty in aircraft testing and development work, again on the forefront of advances in his chosen profession. This type of duty culminated in four years of service as Chief of the Bureau of Aeronautics, responsible for the development and acquisition of new aircraft for the Navy. During that period of duty, from 1947 to 1951, the Navy moved into the field of jet aircraft and was also experimenting with guided missiles. Admiral Pride was the first U.S. Navy flag officer to fly a jet plane.

Even though his engineering training was frequently called upon in development projects, Admiral Pride continued to serve as a line officer and particularly enjoyed the opportunities to command. In this capacity, he commanded a fighter squadron in the 1930s, served as executive officer of the carrier Saratoga at the outbreak of World War II, and put the light carrier Belleau Wood into commission as her first skipper in 1943. He was involved in combat operations in those two ships and later while on the staff of Vice Admiral Richmond Kelly Turner during the conquest of Okinawa in 1945. After the war, Admiral Pride derived satisfaction from commanding carrier divisions that deployed to the Sixth Fleet in the Mediterranean, and from 1953 to 1955 he was Commander Seventh Fleet in the Western Pacific.

Throughout the pages which follow, Admiral Pride recalls his experience with a becoming sense of modesty. He does not dwell, for example, on the fact that he was the first former enlisted man to rise to the rank of vice admiral without benefit of being graduated from the Naval Academy. He puts down to luck his numerous achievements on behalf of the Navy, even though those achievements required a great deal of skill and imagination. And he was truly lucky in a number of instances, most notably in surviving a spectacular airplane crash without loss of life or limb. He was one day away from having part of his leg amputated when a new surgeon came along and implemented a procedure for saving the leg. That made the difference between Pride retiring as a lieutenant commander or a four-star admiral.

The existence of this oral history is the result of the work of Peter Spectre, who did the initial interviews

Pride Preface--Page 3

when he was a member of the Naval Institute staff in 1970. He left for other work before he was able to complete the series, so the final interview was not done until 1984, at which time Admiral Pride was 86. Ever the gentleman, Admiral Pride was most cooperative in doing the final interview and providing corrections and additional information when the entire transcript was presented to him. The words that follow are substantially as spoken, although some changes have been made in the interests of accuracy, clarity, and smoothness. The sequence of some questions and answers has been changed so that the story may be told essentially in chronological fashion as events occurred during the admiral's career. The smooth-typing of the transcript was done by Mr. William Lively.

> Paul Stillwell
> Director of Oral History
> U.S. Naval Institute
> December 1984

ALFRED MELVILLE PRIDE
ADMIRAL, U.S. NAVY (RETIRED)

Born in Somerville, Massachusetts, on 10 September 1897, Admiral Pride served as a machinist's mate, later an ensign, in the Naval Reserve Flying Corps in England and France during World War I. He subsequently transferred to the U.S. Navy and as an aviator was attached to various naval air stations, the aircraft carriers Langley and Lexington, and for two years commanded Fighting Squadron Three based on the Langley. Prior to World War II, he served in the Navy Department's Bureau of Aeronautics and a year each as air officer of the seaplane tender Wright and on the staff of Commander Patrol Wing One, based at San Diego.

At the outbreak of war, he was at sea as executive officer of the carrier Saratoga. After brief duty in 1942 in the Bureau of Aeronautics, he assumed command of the USS Belleau Wood at her commissioning on 31 March 1943. Under his command the carrier participated in numerous operations in the Pacific in 1943-1944 and was awarded the Presidential Unit Citation for extraordinary heroism in action. He received a letter of commendation, with combat "V," from the Commander in Chief Pacific Fleet.

He commanded the Naval Air Center, Pearl Harbor, and naval air bases of the 14th Naval District from March 1944 to April 1945, and for meritorious conduct as Commander Air Support Control Unit, Amphibious Forces, Pacific Fleet from 18 April to 15 October 1945, was awarded the Legion of Merit with combat "V." In January 1946, he reported as officer in charge of the Material Control Branch, Office of the Assistant Secretary of the Navy, and from October 1946 until April 1947 commanded Carrier Division Six and then Carrier Division Four.

Admiral Pride served as Chief of the Bureau of Aeronautics from March 1947 until May 1951, and after a year as Commander Carrier Division Two, assumed command of the Naval Air Test Center, Patuxent River, Maryland. Detached in November 1953 for duty in the Far East, he reported in December as Commander Seventh Fleet. For exceptionally meritorious service in that command until December 1955, he was awarded the Distinguished Service Medal, the citation stating that in the evacuation of the Tachen Islands in February 1955, he "personally supervised and directed the removal of [approximately 27,000] civilians and military personnel and 8,600 tons of military equipment and supplies within a period of three and one-half days [and was] directly responsible and highly successful in implementing U.S. policy in cooperation with the Government of the Republic of China in defense of Taiwan. . ."

On 1 February 1956, he assumed command of the Naval Air Force, U.S. Pacific Fleet. "For exceptionally meritorious conduct. . ." in that capacity he was awarded a gold star in lieu of a second Distinguished Service Medal. On 1 October 1959, Admiral Pride was transferred to the retired list of the U.S. Navy.

PERSONAL DATA:

Born: Somerville, Massachusetts, 10 September 1897
Parents: Alfred Morine Pride and Mrs. Grace (White) Pride
Wife's Name and Date of Marriage: Helen Burrell, 1 June 1921
Children: Carol S. (Pride) Lemeshewsky & Captain Alfred M. Pride, USN (Retired)
Official Address: Dover-Foxcroft, Maine
Education: Public and High Schools, Somerville, Massachusetts; Tufts College Engineering School, Medford, Massachusetts; Postgraduate Aeronautical Engineering School, U.S. Naval Academy, Annapolis, Maryland and Massachusetts Institute of Technology, Cambridge; Flight Training (1918)

PROMOTIONS:

Enlisted service, reserve 20 March 1917 to 8 April 1917
Enlisted service, active 8 April 1917 to September 1918
Commissioned Ensign, USNRF, 17 September 1918
Lieutenant (jg), 1 April 1919
Lieutenant, 1 July 1920
Lieutenant, USN, 29 November 1921
Lieutenant Commander, 1 July 1931
Commander, 23 June 1938
Captain (T), 11 September 1942
Rear Admiral (T) 30 March 1944
Rear Admiral, 7 August 1947, to rank from 5 July 1943
Vice Admiral, 9 October 1953
Transferred to Retired List, 1 October 1959, advanced to Admiral on basis of combat awards

DECORATIONS AND MEDALS:

Distinguished Service Medal
Gold Star in lieu 2nd Distinguished Service Medal
Legion of Merit with Combat "V"
Letter of Commendation with Ribbon and Combat "V"
Presidential Unit Citation with Combat "V" (USS Belleau Wood)
World War I Victory Medal
American Defense Service Medal, Fleet Clasp
Asiatic-Pacific Campaign Medal with silver star (five engagements)
American Campaign Medal
World War II Victory Medal
China Service Medal (extended)
National Defense Service Medal
Korean Service Medal
United Nations Service Medal
Philippine Liberation Ribbon
Korean Presidential Unit Citation

Admiral A. M. Pride, USN (Retired)

Distinguished Service Medal: "For exceptionally meritorious service to the Government of the United States in a duty of great responsibility as Commander Seventh Fleet from December 1953 to December 1955. During the latter months of 1954 when the Seventh Fleet was repeatedly under orders to prepare to support the defenders of the Tachen Islands, he was instrumental in maintaining the Fleet in a high state of combat readiness...He personally supervised and directed the removal of more than 15,600 civilians, 11,100 military personnel and 8,600 tons of military equipment and supplies within a period of three and one-half days...[He] has been directly responsible and highly successful in implementing United States policy in cooperation with the Government of the Republic of China for the defense of Taiwan..."

Gold Star in lieu of the Second Distinguished Service Medal: For exceptionally meritorious service...as Commander Naval Air Force, U.S. Pacific Fleet from January 30, 1956 to October 1, 1959. Since receiving his Navy wings in 1918, Vice Admiral Pride has played an illustrious role in the phenomenal evolution of naval aviation...As Commander Naval Air Force, U.S. Pacific Fleet, [he] has exercised operational planning and administrative ability to the highest caliber; has been eminently successful in carrying out his many and exacting assignments...[and] has made significant contributions to the readiness of his operating forces...His highly trained, combat-ready units are and have been the potent tools which have enabled the cognizant military commands in the Far East to implement the United States national policy, deter aggressor nations, and maintain stability in this strategic area..."

Legion of Merit with Combat "V": "For exceptionally meritorious conduct in the performance of outstanding services to the Government of the United States as Commander Air Support Control Units, Amphibious Forces, United States Pacific Fleet, during operations against enemy Japanese forces on Okinawa Shima, Ryukyu Islands, from April 18 to September 2, 1945...[He] skillfully coordinated and administered the numerous functions of his command and contributed greatly to the success of his air support unit in destroying enemy gun emplacements, troop concentrations and equipment...He provided effective and important air protection for all Fleet units in the assault area [and] aided materially in successfully completing this hazardous campaign..."

Letter of Commendation with Ribbon and Combat "V" (CinCPac): For distinguished service...in action during the operations against the Japanese bases at Tinian, Saipan and Guam in the Marianas on 22 February 1944. In this section for the first time in the war in the Pacific, a Carrier Task Force was discovered by the enemy and obliged to fight its way to its objective...The excellence of his performance in the execution of his duties contributed greatly to the success of our mission...

Presidential Unit Citation (USS Belleau Wood): "For extraordinary heroism in action against enemy Japanese forces in the air, ashore and afloat in the Pacific War Area from September 18, 1943 to August 15, 1945. Spearheading the concentrated carrier warfare in forward areas, the Belleau Wood and her air groups struck crushing blows toward annihilating Japanese fighting power; they provided air cover for our amphibious forces; they fiercely countered the enemy's aerial attacks and destroyed his planes; and they inflicted terrific losses on the Japanese in Fleet and merchant marine units sunk or damaged..."

CHRONOLOGICAL TRANSCRIPT OF SERVICE:

Mar 1917 - Sep 1918	Various assignments as Machinist's Mate 2/c and Chief Quartermaster
Sep 1918 - Jan 1919	Various stations in France and United States as Ensign (Naval Aviator)
Jan 1919 - Oct 1919	Naval Air Station, Chatham, Massachusetts (Ordnance Officer)
Oct 1919 - Dec 1919	Carlstrom Field, Arcadia, Florida (duty under training on land machines)
Dec 1919 - Apr 1922	Naval Air Station, Hampton Roads, Virginia; Atlantic Fleet Ship Plane Division; USS Arizona (Various duties concerning test- and development)
Apr 1922 - Jun 1924	USS Langley (Testing and developing flight deck gear)
Jun 1924 - Jun 1925	Naval Academy, Annapolis, Maryland. Post-graduate school (Aeronautical Engineering instruction)
Jun 1925 - Jul 1926	Massachusetts Institute of Technology, Cambridge, Massachusetts (instruction)
Sep 1926 - Oct 1926	USS Saratoga (commissioning and fitting out)
Nov 1926 - Aug 1929	USS Lexington (first cfo, later Watch and Division officer and Pilot)

Aug 1929 - Jun 1932	Naval Air Station, Norfolk, Virginia (Officer in Charge, Experimental Detachment)
Jul 1932 - Jun 1934	USS Langley, Fighting Squadron Three B (CO) (CO of Bombing Squadron Five A, one month)
Jun 1934 - Jun 1936	Naval Air Station, D.C. (Officer in Charge, Flight Test)
Jun 1936 - Jun 1937	Bureau of Aeronautics, Navy Department, Washington, D.C. (Fighter Desk)
Jun 1937 - Oct 1938	USS Wright (Air Officer)
Oct 1938 - Jun 1939	Patrol Wing One (Operations Officer on Staff)
Jun 1939 - Apr 1941	Bureau of Aeronautics (Navy Working Member on Aeronautical Board)
May 1941 - Jun 1942	USS Saratoga (Executive Officer)
Jun 1942 - Jun 1942	Officer of Procurement and Material, Navy Department
Jun 1942 - Dec 1942	Bureau of Aeronautics, Navy Department
Jan 1943 - Apr 1944	USS Belleau Wood (commissioning and fitting out, then Commanding Officer)
Apr 1944 - Sep 1944	U.S. Naval Air Center, Pearl Harbor, Hawaii (CO)
Sep 1944 - Mar 1945	Naval Air Bases, Fourteenth Naval District (CO)
Apr 1945 - Dec 1945	Air Support Control Units, Amphibious Force, Pacific Fleet (CO)
Jan 1946 - Nov 1946	Office of Assistant Secretary of the Navy (Officer in Charge, Material Control Branch, Material Division)
Dec 1946 - Jan 1947	Carrier Division Six (Commander)
Jan 1947 - Mar 1947	Carrier Division Four (Commander)
Mar 1947 - May 1951	Bureau of Aeronautics, Navy Department (Chief of Bureau)
May 1951 - Apr 1952	Carrier Division Two (Commander)
May 1952 - Nov 1953	Naval Air Test Center, Patuxent River, Maryland (Commander)
Dec 1953 - Dec 1955	Commander Seventh Fleet
Feb 1956 - Sep 1959	Commander Air Force, Pacific Fleet
1 Oct 1959	Retired

Authorization

The U.S. Naval Institute is hereby authorized to make available to libraries and other repositories of its choosing the transcripts of four oral history interviews concerning the life and career of the undersigned. The four interviews were recorded on 24 January, 7 February, and 18 April 1970 in collaboration with Peter Spectre, and on 12 January 1984 in collaboration with Paul Stillwell of the U.S. Naval Institute.

The undersigned does hereby release and assign to the U.S. Naval Institute all right, title, restrictions, and interest in these four interviews. The copyright in both the oral and transcribed versions shall be the sole property of the U.S. Naval Institute. The tape recordings of the interviews are and will remain the property of the U.S. Naval Institute.

Signed and sealed this 21st day of November, 1984.

Alfred M. Pride
Admiral, U. S. Navy (Retired)

Interview Number 1 with Admiral Alfred Melville Pride,
U.S. Navy (Retired)

Place: Admiral Pride's home in Arlington, Virginia

Date: 24 January 1970

Subject: Biography

Interviewer: Peter Spectre

Q: Admiral, could you tell me a little bit about your early background, please?

Admiral Pride: I was born and raised in Somerville, Massachusetts. Upon completion of high school, I entered Tufts Engineering School.

Q: When you were in high school, were you definitely preparing to go to college?

Admiral Pride: Yes, I took the engineering preparatory course. I hadn't decided what school I was going to, but I knew definitely it would be engineering.

Q: What made you go in that direction?

Admiral Pride: I suppose it was a natural bent. My father was a contractor. I worked all of my spare time and summers as a mechanic on his jobs. It never occurred to me that I would be anything but an engineer. I think I was rather mechanically inclined.

Q: What type of contracting work did your father do?

Admiral Pride: Building houses and stores. He was a building contractor.

Q: What about your mother? Was she a housewife?

Admiral Pride: Yes. My mother came from Somerville; her parents were from Maine. My father was born in Nova Scotia.

Q: Did you have any difficulty in getting into Tufts?

Admiral Pride: No, it was pretty much standard procedure. Plus in those days there weren't as many applicants for schools as there are now. It was probably much easier to get into advanced school. College entrance examinations were just coming in in most schools.

Q: What year was it you entered Tufts?

Pride #1 -3-

Admiral Pride: 1916

Q: In engineering--did you specialize in any particular area, such as mechanical engineering?

Admiral Pride: No, I wanted to be a structural engineer which was almost synonymous with civil engineering. In fact, all the engineering courses, at that time, were started off the same. We began to branch out slightly in the second year. All mathematics were completed in the first two years. Chemistry was general too. You had a good start for any engineering specialty that you wished to take on.

Q: Did you have any difficulties with the courses, or were you particularly strong in any area?

Admiral Pride: Yes, I was weak in chemistry.

Q: That seems to be everybody's weakness, I think. It was mine as well.

Admiral Pride: You can't see anything. You can see a

Pride #1 -4-

structure; you can see a piece of mechanism that you design. But most of chemistry in the early stages, you're taking somebody's word for something.

Q: Did you think anything of airplanes, aviation during this period?

Admiral Pride: No, only the general interest that youngsters had at that time. I had been to the Harvard-Boston Aeromeet in 1910 and '11 at Quincy. And, as usual with boys at that time, I made a few models. It never occurred to me that I would be an aviator.

Q: What was the meet like?

Admiral Pride: They had all the famous aviators of those days--Lincoln Beachey, and I think Farnham was there.* I'm not sure. They had the old stick-and-wire airplanes. I remember Beachey, I think it was, flew from Quincy where the meet was held down to Boston Light and back. This was

---
*Lincoln Beachey was a pioneer stunt pilot who first achieved fame for an airship flight around the Washington Monument in 1906. He was killed in an aircraft accident in 1915.

a distance of seven miles each way, and from which he got a very large prize. To fly seven miles was quite a trip.

I can remember being especially interested in the Bleriot monoplane, such as flew across the English Channel.* There were several old types there, and inevitably a Wright plane.

It was quite interesting that several years later--I guess it was in 1920--I flew a Jenny up from Mitchel Field where we were stationed at the time, to Boston.** At that time, there was no airport in Boston. I landed in the old racetrack at Saugus, Massachusetts. Just looking around, I went in alongside the old racetrack. There were several of the old airplanes that had been at Squantum. There was an Antoinette monoplane and several of the others. I've often wondered what has ever become of those old aircraft.

Q: I wonder if they are still there?

Admiral Pride: No, Saugus is all built up now. The racetrack isn't there.

Q: When did you graduate from Tufts?

---
*Louis Bleriot was a French aviation pioneer who made the first aerial crossing of the English Channel on 25 July 1909.
**Jenny was the nickname of the Curtiss JN biplane.

Pride #1 -6-

Admiral Pride: I didn't graduate. I graduated from high school in June. I went there only part of one year. When I was in my freshman year, about March of '17, some lieutenant--I've often wondered who he might have been--came out from the navy yard at Charlestown and urged us to join the Naval Reserve. Because the war was going on in Europe, and we would undoubtedly be getting into it. So that seemed like a good idea, and I went into the navy yard.

Q: How did you come to that decision?

Admiral Pride: I knew if we were going into the war, I would undoubtedly be in it, and I wanted to be in the Navy. All my ancestry was seagoing. My grandfather used to build ships, schooners, in Nova Scotia. He'd sail on a voyage or two, and then sell them, go back and build another. My father went to sea when he was 16 years old. I just felt that I wanted to be in the Navy.

Q: So you joined, actually intending to go into the seagoing service, rather than flying?

Admiral Pride: Oh, yes. I had no idea of being an aviator.

Q: What did your parents have to say?

Admiral Pride: Father said, "If that's what he wants to do, he should do it." So I went into the Boston Navy Yard and told them that I wanted to enlist in the Naval Reserve.

Somebody said, "What do you want to be?"

I said, "I don't know what the ranks or ratings are in the Navy. I'm an engineering student--I suppose some sort of an engineer."

This fellow said, "What's a piston ring made out of?"

I said, "Steel."

He said, "No, cast iron. You're a machinist's mate second class."

I said, "That's fine." So there I was, a machinist's mate second class.

Q: Did you have any basic training?

Admiral Pride: No, we had evening classes for Naval Reserve ratings over at MIT one or two evenings a week.*

Q: Were you a full-time Naval Reservist, or were you on active duty?

---

*MIT--Massachusetts Institute of Technology

Admiral Pride: I was not on active duty until the war started.

Q: You were still in college?

Admiral Pride: I was still in college.

I suppose you're going to ask how I got into active duty, which you can scarcely prevent me from telling you.

War was declared, as I remember, on April 6th. I hadn't been called to the colors, which I thought was an oversight. I was mulling this over when I was in a chemistry lecture on the morning of the 7th. I said to myself, "There's an examination coming up, and you're not going to make it." I walked out of the lecture hall.

In those days, the trolley car came right by the door. On came the trolley car, headed for Charlestown. I said, "I think I'd better go in and see if they don't want to put me on active duty." I got on the trolley car and went in.

They said, "Certainly." And I stayed on active duty until I retired.

Q: You were a chief quartermaster at one time. How did you get from machinist's mate to quartermaster?

Admiral Pride: When I went to active duty--as I say--which was the day after war was declared, they sent me over to where they were establishing a receiving ship on Commonwealth Pier. It was called a receiving ship; it was actually Commonwealth Pier in Boston. I was sent over there.

I had enlisted in some class in the reserve that would head me up for being some sort of an engineer in small craft; I've forgotten what the class was now. They were fitting out yachts and private boats for patrol work, and I was assigned to be the engineer on a converted boat. She was called the Wild Goose.*

Q: This had been a private yacht?

Admiral Pride: Yes. We were assigned to patrol the submarine nets at the entrances to Boston Harbor. That, to me, didn't seem to be a very active participation in the war.

I began to see these airplanes flying out from Naval Air Station Squantum. I thought, "Now there's a

---

*The USS Wild Goose was a 60-foot wooden-hulled screw motorboat which had been built in 1913. She was taken over by the Navy on 21 June 1917 and commissioned on 25 June of that year. After World War I, she was disposed of by the Navy on 17 November 1920.

good business to be in. So when I was home one day, I sat down at my father's typewriter and typed a letter from A. M. Pride, machinist's mate second class, USNR, to somebody I'd heard about called the Chief of Naval Operations. I didn't know just who he was. In this letter, I requested that I be ordered to aviation duty and training as a naval aviator. I went up and put it in the mailbox.

To my astonishment and gratification, after a while the thing came back to me on the <u>Wild Goose</u> directing me to resubmit my request via "official channels." Somebody had stamped on the bottom of the thing, "Approved." Sort of a red stamp "Approved."

So I had my skipper endorse it. I had to go over to the navy yard again, and somebody over there endorsed it. And the thing went through.

I was ordered to aviation training at MIT and later at Miami.

Q: That was ground school?

Admiral Pride: Ground school was at MIT. Miami was the flight school.

Q: What did you study there?

Admiral Pride: Theory of flight--that is, why an airplane flies. Nobody's too certain about that yet. Inevitably, Navy Regulations, in those days we had Naval Instructions too, which was a pretty good book. It didn't have the force of regulations, but it told you what you ought to do. Signaling, an awful lot of dot-dash code. Inevitably, calisthenics and close-order drill.

Q: Did you find it worthwhile?

Admiral Pride: Oh, yes. For one thing, they had very strict discipline. A fellow named Cabaniss was in command there.* He was a very strict disciplinarian, which was an awfully good thing. Because many of us--we were called cadets--had never been in the military environment before. They whipped us into shape very fast.

I submitted this request in the summertime. A strange thing, it seemed to me, was along in late autumn the Navy Department decided that it didn't need all the reserves it had on that kind of duty. If we were in a college course, they sent us back to our colleges. I went

---

*Lieutenant Robert W. Cabaniss, USN, naval aviator number 36, who was killed in a plane crash in 1927. Cabaniss Field at Corpus Christi, Texas, was dedicated in his honor in July 1941.

back to Tufts for about three months. But then I got my orders to MIT.

Q: How long did you spend at MIT?

Admiral Pride: I think it was about 12 weeks; I'm not sure of that. Then I went to Miami--we had a naval air station there--for my elementary flying. Then I went over to Pensacola for about six weeks, I think. Then I was shipped over to France. I had been there but a very short time when the war ended.

Q: When were you commissioned--after you left MIT?

Admiral Pride: Upon graduation from the advanced flying course at Pensacola. I think that was in September.

Q: Can you tell me something about what type of training you had in Miami and Pensacola?

Admiral Pride: The very rudiments of flying in Miami. We were taken out and taught how to handle the plane in the air, how to make landings and takeoffs.

Pride #1 -13-

Q: What type of aircraft did you use?

Admiral Pride: They had an assortment of aircraft there. There were some Aeromarines, one or two Thomas seaplanes. They had some R-6s--which were considered large--Curtiss aircraft with an abominable engine, Curtiss V-2 engine. There were one or two Thomas Scouts, but the students were not permitted to fly those. There were some things called MF boats.

Q: Were there a lot of students there?

Admiral Pride: I suppose there were 400 or 500, thinking of the size of the barracks and so forth.

Q: How many were in your particular group?

Admiral Pride: Of the contingent that went to Miami from MIT, I would say no more than probably 25 or 30.

Q: Did everybody make it through?

Admiral Pride: We had several casualties. A few were busted out; not very many busted out.

Q: When you speak of casualties, you're talking about accidents?

Admiral Pride: Fatalities.

Q: What about at Pensacola? What type of training did you have there? When was the first time you did your solo, at Miami?

Admiral Pride: At Miami. You didn't go to Pensacola until you soloed. I was rather slow at it; I was five hours and 45 minutes before soloing. Some real bright ones would be able to solo in about five hours, but not very many. Some went up to 10 or 12 hours before they soloed. If you didn't solo when you got 10 or 12 hours in, you were getting to be looked at with considerable doubt. I think probably the average was around five or six hours.

Q: At Pensacola, you went into advanced training.

Admiral Pride: So-called. They had two-engine flying boats there. Looking back, I think we were taking quite a chance, because they were short of what they called gunnery pilots. They were simply pilots to fly students over the bombing range while they dropped their bombs. They put me on that work for a while. I don't suppose I had 30 hours in, when I was doing that. The fellow in the back seat was probably taking quite a chance.

Q: Then you were sent over to France.

Admiral Pride: Then I went to France, a place called Moutchic.

Q: What type of duty did you have there?

Admiral Pride: We flew flying boats that were over there for patrol work. What we were actually doing was being prepared for actual antisubmarine patrols off the French coast. While I was still there, the war ended. So I only got in one or two patrols.

Q: What did you think about aviation in general, after getting into it? Did you see a future in it?

Admiral Pride: Oh, sure, I loved it. It was pretty hard

Pride #1 -16-

to be in at all without being very enthusiastic about it. Being a youngster, it was a whole new environment. There was a lot of satisfaction in just flying an aircraft. You felt that you were rather egotistical about it. You felt you were one of the privileged.

Q: What happened to you after the war ended?

Admiral Pride: When the war was over, I was still a reserve. And we were ordered to the stations nearest our homes in the United States until it was determined what should be done with us.

We had a coastal air station at Chatham, Massachusetts, so that was the one that I was ordered to. While there, I learned that the Navy was about to fly aircraft off of the battleships for spotting gunfire. I don't know how I found out about that, but I thought I'd like to try that.

Q: Didn't it scare you?

Admiral Pride: Not particularly. So I wrote another letter, this time via channels, and asked to be assigned to this duty. Which I was and ordered to Carlstrom Field in Florida, which was an Air Corps station. There I joined what was to become the Atlantic Fleet Ship Plane Division.

Q: Is this when you integrated into the regular Navy?

Admiral Pride: No, we weren't transferred over to the regular Navy until 1921. See, this was happening in 1919.

This group at Carlstrom Field was under the command of Godfrey Chevalier.* Have you come across his name before?

Q: I think I have.

Admiral Pride: Very important name in this part of aviation.

I think there were 16 of us that were assigned to this duty. The Air Corps were to teach us to fly land planes. Of course, these people were all contemporaries of ours, the Air Corps people. They started us right in, as though we had never seen an airplane before--that is,

---

*Lieutenant Commander Godfrey deC. Chevalier, USN, naval aviator number 7.

through the Air Corps's elementary training. This was rather hard on our egos, because very few of them had been on duty in Europe during the war, and most all of us had been.

Q: You had never flown a land plane before?

Admiral Pride: I had never flown a land plane until then. They put us right through their elementary training, and then their advanced training. We got into their single-engine fighters, then were turned loose to go to our destined battleships. I was ordered to the Arizona.

Q: Why were you trained in land-based airplanes?

Admiral Pride: We had no land planes in the Navy, except for the few we had used in the Northern Bombing Group and a few here and there on special projects.* So they had to teach us to fly land planes, because we were to fly land planes off the battleships.

We were to use, on the forward turrets, something

---

*The Northern Bombing Group was a U. S. aviation organization which operated in France near the end of World War I.

called Sopwith Strut and a Half, which was a two-seated airplane. On the after turrets, we had Nieuport 28s.

Q: Can you tell me something in detail about how the project got started on the Arizona? Were you in at the beginning?

Admiral Pride: Some experiments had been made, I think, on the Texas the previous winter. What had happened was that Chevalier, Whiting, and others who were influential in naval aviation had watched the British experiments in flying off of ships for this purpose, to scout for the ships and spot their gunfire.* Chevalier went over to Britain and observed there the tests that they were making. Our Navy Department thought this was a pretty good idea. Because, you see, our aerial observation at that time from the battleships was confined to the use of kite balloons. They obviously couldn't go out on scouting trips, couldn't leave the ship. They were moored to the ship. So the Navy Department thought this was a pretty good idea and made some tests on the Texas in which they built a platform on the guns of the number two turret, the

---

*Commander Kenneth Whiting, USN, naval aviator number 16.

high turret. Then they had the airplane take off on this little runway.*

Q: How did they get the planes back?

Admiral Pride: We landed on the beach, wherever we could find a field and towed the airplane by anything we could. I used an ox team in Cuba, down to the shore. These planes weren't very heavy. We got them onto a 50-foot motor launch and brought them back out and hoisted them back on the ship with a boat crane.

The platforms were made of the painting stages which all the battleships carried. The framework could be assembled very quickly on top of the guns. By the time I got to the Arizona, they used both the number two and three turrets.

---

*On 9 March 1919, Lieutenant Commander E. O. McDonnell, USN, flying a Sopwith Camel, made the first flight from a turret platform on a U.S. Navy battleship as he successfully took off from the number two turret of the USS Texas (BB-35), lying at anchor at Guantanamo. Subsequently a VE-7 was launched from a compressed air catapult on the USS Maryland (BB-46) on 24 May 1922. A powder catapult was successfully demonstrated in the launching of a Martin MO-1 from the forward turret of the USS Mississippi (BB-41) on 14 December 1924. Following the Mississippi demonstration, the powder catapult was widely used on battleships and cruisers.

Q: How big was the runway?

Admiral Pride: It was 52 feet long, as I remember. Which meant that you had to have a pretty good breeze blowing down the line of the runway to be sure to get you in the air before you struck the water. In fact, we had two or three of them go in the water. Then we arrived through experience at the notion that you had to have at least 22 knots of wind down the runway. That meant that with the number three turret--the battleship had a speed of about 20-22 knots--you had to get a fairly good breeze blowing. Then the ship would be steaming almost across the wind to make the apparent wind come down the deck.

I flew off number three turret, because that was a single seater and I was the senior of the two aviators. The single seaters were always thought to be more desirable; I don't know why. They were more lively, more maneuverable. We put the tail up on a horse and restrained the plane with a pelican hook, then revved the engine up full.* You nodded your head, and somebody released the pelican hook. Down the platform you went,

---
*A pelican hook is a quick-release device shaped somewhat like a pelican's beak.

hoping to God that you'd get flying speed before you got to the water. You always barely made it, if you made it at all.

Q: Did you ever miss?

Admiral Pride: I never went in the water that way. I've been in the water several times, but I never failed to take off from the turret.

Q: Who else flew with you off the Arizona?

Admiral Pride: A fellow named Wolfer was the other pilot.* He was from up in Pennsylvania. He was killed the following year; he spun in down in Guantanamo Bay.

Q: Where did you conduct the experiments?

Admiral Pride: I joined the ship from her home yard, which was the Brooklyn Navy Yard. Then we left for Guantanamo within a week or two. We did most of this work off Guantanamo.

---

*Lieutenant (junior grade) Jacob F. Wolfer, USNRF.

The planes that we had--the Nieuports were French planes, which I think we got in exchange for some motor trucks. The Sopwith Strut and a Half were British planes. Both of them had rotary engines, which sometimes were rather unreliable.

Q: What did the non-aviators think of all this?

Admiral Pride: Very little. I caught hell, because the rotary engine used castor oil. It would spew out, and drops of it would go down on the beautiful teak on the quarterdeck of the Arizona.

When I reported in, the skipper of that battleship was a very fine man. But he told me that he didn't believe in airplanes on ships.* And that the only future for aviation in the fleet that he could see was small dirigibles towed by the battleships. They could cast them loose and go out and scout and come back to another ship. I think that they appreciated our spotting very much, but they regretted these damn dirty airplanes on their ships.

---
*Captain John H. Dayton, USN, was commanding officer of the Arizona (BB-39), when Lieutenant (junior grade) Pride reported aboard in 1920.

Pride #1 -24-

Q: Actually, what you were doing was more operational work than experimental work.

Admiral Pride: Yes, the experimental work had been pretty well done in the previous year on the Texas.

Q: So that your mission was a secondary mission as far as the ship was concerned.

Admiral Pride: They were awfully glad to have us there in the long-range firing, because we could do so much more accurate spotting than they could from the ship.

Q: What I mean is that the Arizona didn't go out on that mission specifically.

Admiral Pride: No, the Arizona would never go to sea for that purpose. She went about her usual business, and we did some of her spotting for her.

Q: How long were you with the Arizona?

Admiral Pride: I was attached to her for a year. Then I was shifted to the Nevada.

Q: For the same type of duty?

Admiral Pride: Yes.

When the ship came back to the navy yard, we assembled out at Mitchel Field.* We borrowed their facilities for that, part of them, from the Air Corps. We spent that summer flying around there to keep our hands in. Then we went back to battleships in the autumn.

Q: This was between the Arizona and the Nevada?

Admiral Pride: No, I spent the first winter in the Arizona and the next winter in the Nevada.

Actually most of the time that we were around Guantanamo, we'd keep the airplanes flying to keep our hands in. We operated from Hicacal Beach over on the west side of Guantanamo Bay. We established a camp there.

Q: Were there other battleships with you?

Admiral Pride: Oh, yes. The Pennsylvania, Arizona, Nevada and Oklahoma had the turrets rigged for the aircraft.

---

*Mitchel Field was at Mineola, Long Island, New York.

Q: So you had an opportunity to exchange notes with the other aviators?

Admiral Pride: We would gather together a great deal in port. As I say, every day we were over at Hicacal Beach flying.

In fact, we had to assemble our aircraft there. We didn't take any planes south with us in the battleships on the first cruise. We got down there and were met by a collier, which had our aircraft aboard in crates. We took those ashore, up over Conde Bluff and down onto the flats, and assembled them ourselves.

Q: Did you work on the actual machinery of the planes?

Admiral Pride: Oh yes, sure, everybody did.

Q: Did you have a ground crew with you?

Admiral Pride: Yes we did, but everybody had to work on it. Most of us had never seen any of these aircraft before. They were all foreign aircraft. Everybody did everything.

Pride #1 -27-

Q: What happened to you after the Nevada?

Admiral Pride: We came back and assembled again at Norfolk Naval Air Station.

Just prior to that, the people who were interested in this business, Chevalier and Whiting particularly, had figured out that we'd better get a carrier in the Navy. So they asked for the Mount Vernon--she'd been the Kronprinzesin Cecilie--because they wanted a big ship.* You needed a large flight deck to operate aircraft from. But they were granted the collier Jupiter. She was sent to the navy yard at Norfolk to be converted into a carrier and named the Langley.

Chevalier told me that I was to stay ashore at Norfolk and devise an arresting gear to stop the aircraft on the Langley's deck. There was no provision for arresting in her original plans. In fact, nobody had figured what to do about that. So I stayed at Norfolk and worked out the arresting gear for the Langley until 1924. I worked on the arresting gear and designed it and saw it installed. When the Langley went into commission in '22, I

---
*A former German liner which had been commissioned by the United States and used as a troop transport during World War I.

Pride #1 -28-

was in their commissioning detail.* I served in her and was detached from her in '24 to go to the Postgraduate School.

Q: What was involved in designing an arresting gear? Was there any previous work done on this?

Admiral Pride: Yes. A civilian aviator named Ely had made a landing on a cruiser out in San Francisco with an old pusher aircraft.** They had built a long platform from her mainmast out over the stern.

To stop the airplane, they hung some hooks on it, and then they put wires across the deck with sandbags. There was a sandbag on each end of each wire, and there were quite a lot of them. So that when he came down and landed, the hooks snagged these wires and dragged more and more of these sandbags and brought him to rest. It seemed such

---

*The USS Langley was commissioned 20 March 1922 at Norfolk, Virginia, under temporary command of her executive officer, Commander Kenneth Whiting, USN. Later in the year, Captain Stafford H. R. Doyle, USN, a non-aviator, took over as commanding officer. For an interesting article on the formative years of the ship, see Rear Admiral Jackson R. Tate, USN(Ret.), "We Rode the Covered Wagon," U. S. Naval Institute Proceedings, October 1978, pages 62-69.

**The first flight to a shipboard deck in the U.S. Navy was made by Eugene Ely, who landed on 18 January 1911 on the stern of the USS Pennsylvania (ARC-4), not to be confused with the battleship Pennsylvania (BB-38).

an obvious way to stop anything that I started out to try and see how this thing was going to work out. I just put sandbags on wires across the roadway down there, to find out how I should design the hook for the planes that we then had.

In the meantime, the Navy Department had built a turntable on the field at Hampton Roads, about 100 feet in diameter, flush with the ground. They mounted on it some gear that the British were then using. That gear was not successful, and they ripped it out. I mounted on the same turntable some crosswires, instead of sandbags, that were going to drag along weights suspended in towers. Then it became much more of an engineering operation. You knew what the plane weighed. You knew about how fast it was coming in, so you knew its kinetic energy. You knew how much weight you had and how high the weights could go, so you knew how much potential energy they were going to have. You could balance those out and come up with a rational prediction of where the airplane was going to stop, how far it was going to run out. Actually, there was such a great loss of friction in the system that the potential energy of the weights at the end of a run was usually only a part of the kinetic energy of the aircraft as it landed. But at least you had a rational approach to the thing. You never knew what you were going to get dragging the sandbags along.

Q: What principle did the British type of gear bring?

Admiral Pride: They simply used some cables stretched real taut about 9 inches apart and a little over a foot off the deck. Our version of it had them 15 inches off the deck. On the axle of the landing gear were these hooks, like anchors, that went down between these longitudinal cables. Just the friction of the cables was supposed to stop you. It never did; your plane went up on its nose at the end of the run. The British called it a Harp or a B-gear. In their version, the wires were high enough so the plane actually rested on them and coasted along on the wires. The friction was much greater.

Q: Didn't that tear up the plane?

Admiral Pride: Yes, busted the propeller in almost every landing. It was disastrous. They never put it into other than experimental use.

Q: Who tested the designs that you came up with?

Admiral Pride: I did.

Q: How did you feel about them? Were you confident that it was going to work?

Admiral Pride: No, every test was a question of whether it would work.

Q: What would happen if you missed, if your hook didn't pick up the cable? Could you just keep on flying?

Admiral Pride: We were shortsighted. We should have discarded the fore-and-aft cables at the very beginning. We didn't discard them, and they put them into the Lexington and Saratoga. It was there that a naval constructor named Stevens said, "Let's do away with those fore-and-aft cables."* They were breaking up more aircraft than they were saving, but there was a great fear of going over the side. The British had used these, because they had had some very disastrous experiences, in

---

*Leslie C. Stevens, who was a lieutenant commander in the Navy's Construction Corps when the Lexington (CV-2) and Saratoga (CV-3) were commissioned in the late 1920s.

their early experiments. Because they were going to have to take off from the ship, they built the platform forward. They used very small, light airplanes, a Sopwith Camel, I think. I flew one of those my second year. They would come in, have to make a very sharp turn in by the foremast and down onto the platform.

There was one of the cruises when they lost some overboard. It was a bad place to go overboard, because the ship ran over you.

So they were very strongly orientated toward the fore-and-aft wires. And we were too, but it began to dawn on us that these things were causing more breakups than they were worth.

To go back to your question--if you were low enough so that your axle hooks engaged the fore-and-aft wires, and your trailing hook did not engage a crosswire, then you came to the end of the fore-and-aft wires, and you went up on your nose.

Q: Did you have any help in your experiments?

Admiral Pride: There were usually two or three other people. I was pretty much on my own, though.

Pride #1   -33-

Q: How did you happen to get this assignment?

Admiral Pride: I haven't any idea. Chevalier walked up to me one day and said, "You make up a gear to stop the airplanes on the Langley." I said, "Aye, aye, Sir." And that's all there was to that.

Q: How long did it take you until you came up with a good design?

Admiral Pride: Not very long, probably not more than five or six months. I had to, because I understood the ship was going into commission in April of '22. This was the start of the summer of '21.

As I would get ideas, I would have to go to Norfolk to tell the draftsmen over there what we'd better put in the ship. I had to work pretty fast.

Q: What was the ultimate design that you came up with for the Langley?

Admiral Pride: The weights obviously were heavy and cumbersome. They had a great advantage that the system was self-contained. If the ship would lose its power, you could still fly airplanes after the wire had been pulled out. You had to get the wire back into battery; the weights took care of that. I had a come-along arrangement. The wire would play out, but then you could control its coming back. The first weights were just blocks of cast iron on the towers that supported the flight deck.

She came back from overhaul a year later, and much better designed weights were put in at Norfolk. They were put down in one of the holds of the ship. However, it was still a bulky and awkward system.

Q: Did it have to be adjusted when a different type of airplane was landed on the deck, say, a heavier airplane flew in after a light airplane?

Admiral Pride: On the first ones that was a distinct disadvantage. The landing area was about 256 feet long. On the earliest design we graduated the weights; the top weight was the lightest and the bottom was the heaviest. A light airplane would drag the thing out aways. When the top weight had moved up a little bit, then it picked up another weight, and so forth. So there was no adjustment. As planes became faster and larger and more diverse in their types, this became necessary.

After I finished the postgraduate course up at MIT, I was ordered to the Lexington to put her in commission. We had this fellow Norden that designed the Norden bombsight.* I talked with him some. He had been engaged to have a much more sophisticated system of stopping the aircraft and one that was adjustable for different weights and speeds of airplanes. Norden had designed this system which used a winch on each end of the crosswire. It was a winch that was hooked into the Waterbury speed gear that put pressure on a big brake. When I'd been on the Lexington a while (I was on her for a couple of years), I was flight deck officer, and there was an inherent difficulty with this gear. If a plane landed off center, it was inclined to go still further off center. In fact, it wanted to go over the side.

Q: You're talking about off the center of the runway?

Admiral Pride: Yes, of the flight deck. Any deviation

---
*Carl L. Norden, a civilian consultant employed by the Navy.

from the center was aggravated as the plane went up the deck. This was a pretty serious thing. Also, it depended on the ship's power to get the gear back into battery for the next aircraft. You had to wind this cable back with an electric motor.

At the end of my cruise on the Lexington, I was ordered back to Norfolk to design another gear that wouldn't have these difficulties. I designed the hydraulic gear that is a much more sophisticated version, but it is the forerunner of the gear that is still used. The basic principle is still the same. That went into the Lexington and the Saratoga to replace the Norden gear.

Q: Can you tell me a little bit about the Langley, some of the problems that you may have encountered?

Admiral Pride: I know a lot about the Langley. Not the least of their problems was the matter of power. She was, I guess, the first electric drive ship in the Navy. And it wasn't too reliable. I remember when we left the navy yard at Norfolk, we went at about six knots out the channel. That's all she'd do. The maximum speed was about 13 knots; you were lucky if you got that.

In later years, in '32 to '34 I guess, I had a fighter squadron on the Langley. I wished she'd go faster many times. But she was a very useful ship. She taught us an awful lot about carrier technique.

Q: Did you fly a lot on board her?

Admiral Pride: Yes. I didn't make the first landing on her. Chevalier made the first landing, and I made the second one. Griffin made the first takeoff.* Of course, I made many, many when I had the squadron on her. There were only about a half a dozen of us that flew from the Langley for some time.

In '23 the Navy wanted to show her off, and we made a cruise. We started at Bar Harbor, Maine. We came down to Portland, Portsmouth, Gloucester, Boston, and New York. All those places we'd anchor out and make landings and takeoffs for the entertainment of the people on the beach. They advertised that we had a carrier. We did all that operation at anchor, of course.

---

*Lieutenant Commander Virgil C. Griffin, Jr., USN, known as "Squash." Griffin made the first takeoff on 17 October 1922 in a Vought VE-7SF while the ship was anchored in the York River. Chevalier, flying an Aeromarine, made the initial landing 26 October 1922 with the Langley under way off Cape Henry.

Q: Why don't we continue our discussion next time; we've covered quite a bit of ground.

Pride #2 -39-

Interview Number 2 with Admiral Alfred Melville Pride,
U.S. Navy (Retired)

Place: Admiral Pride's home in Arlington, Virginia

Date: 7 February 1970

Subject: Biography

Interviewer: Peter Spectre

Q: Admiral, the last time that we spoke, we were talking about the Langley. It was just put in commission and you did a voyage down the eastern coast of the United States. Could you tell me a little bit more, please?

Admiral Pride: We spent that summer shaking down--the summer, autumn, and part of the winter. Then in the springtime of '23--it was late spring-early summer--we started this cruise to publicize the Navy's carrier. There were about six of us who were qualified to operate-- to land and take off and fly from the ship.

Q: Do you remember the names?

Admiral Pride: There was Boatswain Daly, Boatswain Feher, Lieutenant Conley, myself, Lieutenant Commander Griffin, and I think there would be one more, but I can't remember.* There were one or two more. Offhand, I can't think just which ones there were.

As I indicated in the previous interview, the routine was to go into a port, anchor in the port, and make the community well aware that we were there. We published the times when we would be making takeoffs and landings, and then go ahead and make them.

The timing coincided with some 150-year celebrations they were having in some of the New England towns. In fact, by the time we got to Washington here, there was a Shriners' convention, which was most fortunate.

Q: When you did your flying in the various ports that you visited, was it just straight flying? Was there an exhibition or a show?

Admiral Pride: No, maybe a little formation flying over the city. The people were mostly interested in the actual landings and takeoffs from the deck of the ship.

Q: What reaction did people have to this?

---

*Boatswain Walter J. Daly, USN; Boatswain Anthony Feher, USN; Lieutenant (junior grade) Delbert L. Conley, USN.

Admiral Pride: Very enthusiastic. It was rather spectacular to see an airplane come to rest in such a short distance and to take off in such a short distance. The takeoffs at anchor, with little or no wind, were usually spectacular, because the plane frequently would not have quite flying speed when it got to the end of the deck and would sink a little. People would wonder how far it was going to go down.

Q: You probably wondered yourself.

Admiral Pride: We had done enough so that we were confident. We had a 52-foot drop from the deck to the water. You'd always get your flying speed in that height.

Q: What type of planes were you flying at that time?

Admiral Pride: We had made our original test landings and takeoffs with Aeromarines, which were light aircraft. You could land and take off at very low speed, in a very short distance.

During the cruise--by that time, we were using Vought VE-7s, which were two-seated airplanes of considerably higher performance. They wouldn't be regarded as having very high performance today, but in those days, they were competitive airplanes.

I had a single seater, SF, that I had been using on test work at Norfolk, but most of the work was done by the Voughts.

Q: Were these airplanes that were built especially for carriers?

Admiral Pride: Oh, no, we had none that were built especially for carriers at that time. They were all aircraft that we had made gear for and installed practically all of it ourselves in the shops at Hampton Roads.

Q: Were you thinking at that time about possibly designing aircraft for carriers?

Admiral Pride: We were thinking about it. What was done was that perfectly conventional aircraft--aircraft that had been designed without the carriers in mind particularly--were modified by having trailing hooks and axle hooks put in. The gear hung on them to adapt them to the carrier work. But no, there was no special design for carrier work. In fact, few came along seriously for several years.

Q: How was your arresting gear working?

Admiral Pride: It worked all right. As I indicated in the previous interview, the weight system was cumbersome; it was heavy in the ship. I wasn't at all satisfied with it. Also, I didn't feel it was as flexible as it needed to be to take care of aircraft that probably would be coming along in the future. At that time, performance of the aircraft and the weight of aircraft were proceeding along pretty predictable lines. The rate at which their performance was increasing and the rate at which their weight was going up were following a pretty predictable curve.

So that we knew in a very short time we were going to have aircraft probably weighing twice as much and landing at appreciably higher speeds. The energy to be absorbed was going up proportionately. In fact, it was going to go up as the square of the landing speed and directly as the weight. So that the weight system of arresting gear was going to reach its limit in a very short time.

Q: You went on this cruise on the eastern seaboard; what happened then to yourself?

Admiral Pride: I was detached from the ship and sent ashore to Norfolk to work on arresting gear for the Lexington and the Saratoga. I stayed there until the spring of '24.

Q: Were you still experimenting with weights, or were you working with more advanced types of gear?

Admiral Pride: I was working on weights and trying to refine that system. But in the back of my mind I began to have notions. There were various other systems; we had quite a number of notions.

Q: Were there other people working with you at this time?

Admiral Pride: I had two or three other pilots with me at Norfolk. I've forgotten just who they were. I worked very closely with opposite numbers in the Bureau of Aeronautics, because I had to get my money from them and made all my reports to them.

Q: Was your design work more theoretical or practical?

Admiral Pride: Both.

Q: Were you adapting things as you went along?

Admiral Pride: Yes, a whole lot of it was improvisation with material and equipment that I could get out of the Navy stock catalog over at the Naval Yard Norfolk or the air station.

Q: Did they support you on this?

Admiral Pride: Yes, there was never any lack of support. But, you see, I had had only about a year of college. I wanted more engineering education very badly. So I had asked to go to the postgraduate school in '23.

Admiral Land was then the head of the Material

Division of the Bureau of Aeronautics.* He told me that he would like to have me stay at Norfolk for another year, and then he would try to see that I went to the postgraduate school, and he did.

I went to the postgraduate school in '24. It was in Annapolis then. The following year I went to MIT.**

Q: What did you study in Annapolis?

Admiral Pride: We had general engineering subjects and toward a specialty, which in my case was aeronautical engineering, which is what I did postgraduate work in at MIT.**

Q: This must have been a fairly new field, aeronautical engineering.

Admiral Pride: MIT probably had the most renowned course in it at that time, although Cal Tech was coming right along.*** Professor Eddie Warner headed up the course at

---

*Captain Emory S. Land, Construction Corps, USN.
**MIT--Massachusetts Institute of Technology
***Cal Tech--California Institute of Technology, Pasadena.

MIT.* He'd had it going, I guess, since World War I. I'm not sure but what that course was going on before the war.

Q: What type of things did you study in the curricula at both postgraduate schools?

Admiral Pride: We started, at Annapolis, with quite a bit of mathematics. Much of it was review for me, because I had had a concentrated course in that at Tufts. Of course, we had physics, hydraulics--and all the basic engineering studies.

Then, at MIT, we concentrated, of course, on aeronautical engineering subjects, structures, and the theory of flight. Much time was spent on review of work that had been done abroad, especially in Germany at the Gottingen Laboratory.

Q: You began your service as an enlisted man. Since you began, up to the period of time we're talking about now, you advanced fairly rapidly. You were assigned fairly good duty, I would imagine, compared to what other people were getting. I'd like to ask you just a general question

---
*Edward P. Warner

about the service of that time. That is: were you an exception in how you advanced--in other words, an enlisted man making officer?

Admiral Pride: Of course, there were many, many enlisted men that obtained their commissions in the reserve force. I would say I was about average for those who applied for some special training, such as aviation or maybe some officer candidate school. If you really wanted to get a commission in the reserve and had any qualification at all, you'd probably get it. Of course, real weeding out came probably after the war, when we were given the chance to transfer to the regular service.

Those examinations were taken in the spring of '21, and we got our commissions in the fall. There were a great many of the reserves that did not want to go for a Navy career. My decision was made for me when I went back to Tufts and found that I was not going to get as much credit as I thought I should have. Also, I would be two years behind my contemporaries in professional life when I graduated. At that age, you don't like that. Later on, it doesn't seem as important, but when you're in your early 20s, it does seem important.

Q: Some of them reverted back?

Admiral Pride: Yes, by far the majority reverted to either ensign or lieutenant (junior grade).

That worked out awfully well for me in later years, because I was either the youngest or next to the youngest man in my rank. There was nobody senior to me who was younger than I--although there was one exception--for many years.* Of course, in the Navy scheme of things, it's advantageous to be young for your rank.

Q: What about when it came time to apply for postgraduate school? Getting a position in postgraduate school is difficult now; it was probably difficult then. Were there any hard feelings or hard work getting this, in light of the fact that you hadn't attended the Naval Academy?

Admiral Pride: No, not at all; there was never any. In fact, it seemed to me that I was getting an extra break.

---

*For purposes of seniority on the lineal list, Pride was placed after members of the Naval Academy's class of 1918 and ahead of those from the class of 1919. Many of the members of the class of 1918 (which was graduated in 1917 because of World War I) were born in 1896 or before; Pride was born on 10 September 1897.

There were quite a number of my classmates at postgraduate school that were not Naval Academy graduates. I should think probably a third of the membership of that class were not Naval Academy graduates. No, I had never seen any sign of any prejudice. I never felt it worked against me at all. In fact, I have sometimes almost suspected the contrary.

Q: When you attended postgraduate school, what was the intention? When you left, was the intention that you'd go into design work or continue as a flier?

Admiral Pride: I wanted to stay in the line distinctly, as a line officer.* I felt deeply interested in engineering and mechanical design. I knew there would always be room for people with such qualifications in the line. And it worked out that way, because that training, although it had become very old, it still stood me in good stead when I was Chief of Bureau of Aeronautics, where

---
*Navy pilots were then either specialized enlisted men or were line officers if commissioned. Those who specialized in aeronautical engineering and design work became members of the Construction Corps. The Construction Corps no longer exists; aircraft design is now done by aeronautical engineering duty officers.

much of my consideration had to be based on engineering judgment.

Q: What happened to you after MIT?

Admiral Pride: I was ordered to the fitting-out detail of the Saratoga at New York Shipbuilding Company, Camden, New Jersey. I had been there but a few months when I was transferred to the fitting-out detail of the Lexington at Quincy, Massachusetts.

Q: Were both ships fitted out with the arresting gear that you had designed before?

Admiral Pride: No. The arresting gear had been devised by Carl Norden, the inventor of the Norden bombsight.

Q: Did he take over where you left off when you went to school?

Admiral Pride: No, he started with an entirely different concept. He designed some very ingenious winches, in which the above-deck equipment still employed wires across the deck that the trailing hooks could engage. Each end of the athwartship wire led to a winch. It was a very ingenious affair. As the wire unreeled from the winch, the winch operated a Waterbury speed gear, which was a pump really, which applied pressure to the brake on the winch. That stopped the aircraft. Then there had to be an electric motor to rewind the winch, to bring the cable back into battery. I didn't like this idea very much, because it seemed to me that if you lost power in the ship, you could no longer land the aircraft. If you had your aircraft all in the air, you were going to lose them all at sea. I'd been in battleships, I'd been in the Langley. I'd seen the ships lose their power. The ship just stopped. This is a casualty that I suspect still happens. It would be very embarrassing if you had all of your aircraft in the air at that time.

So I wanted to get back to a self-contained system, one that would keep on landing airplanes, whether the ship had any power or not. That's why I dreamed up this hydraulic system, which uses the energy of the plane in landing to retrieve the system and get it back in battery. As it drags the wire out, it builds up pressure in the hydraulic system, which is used to pull the wire back into battery for the next airplane.

Pride #2 -53-

Q: Does this all happen after the airplane has been unhooked from the wire?

Admiral Pride: Yes.

Q: Does it have to be done very quickly?

Admiral Pride: There's only a few seconds until the next airplane's coming in. Yes, it has to be done quickly.

Q: Were you landing airplanes at this time, while the ship was under way?

Admiral Pride: Yes. When we weren't having our shows for the people on the beaches, we operated under way all the time from the early days of the Langley. In fact, the first landing that was made on the Langley was made by Chevalier, and the ship was under way at the time.

Q: You spoke about working on the commissioning details of both aircraft carriers. What did that entail?

Admiral Pride: Mostly inspection work. It was largely

watching the installation going in. Although the inspection was the responsibility of the resident Navy inspector, to whom incidentally I reported for duty, nevertheless, most of the aviation equipment inspection was detailed to those of us who were aviators.

Then the ship's air department organization had to be written up. We did a lot of work on safety orders in connection, not only with the aircraft, but with the aircraft fuel systems.

Inevitably, in these new designs, as things actually took shape, changes were necessary that had not been evident on the drawings.

Q: Did you have the authority to make these changes yourself?

Admiral Pride: No, because that would involve cost, you see. We recommended them. If they were minor, the resident naval inspector would possibly authorize them. But most everything had to come back to the Navy Department for approval.

Q: Did you have any lessons that you learned in the

Pride #2 -55-

Langley that you applied to the Lexington and the Saratoga when you commissioned them?

Admiral Pride: Oh yes, many of them.

Q: Could you tell me about some of them?

Admiral Pride: Yes, one was a very amusing one. In the previous interview, did I mention carrier pigeons?

Q: No.

Admiral Pride: Up to the time the Langley was commissioned, every naval air station had carrier pigeons. We used to take these on flights. Before you started on your flight, you went over to the pigeon loft and got your little box with four pigeons in it. You took them along with you. Then, if you had a forced landing, of which we had quite a number, you wrote your message, out where you were, on the piece of paper and stuck it in the capsule that was fastened to the pigeon's leg and let it go. It flew back to the air station, and they knew where you were, presumably. This had been going on for a long while in the very early days of aviation.

So just on the fantail of the <u>Langley</u> was a room half again as large as this one that was the pigeon loft. We went into the Chesapeake Bay and anchored off Tangier Island to shake down. The pigeon quartermaster--there was such a fellow--would let his pigeons out, one or two at a time, for exercise. They'd leave the ship and fly around, and they usually stayed in sight. Pretty soon they'd come back and land. There was a little alarm bell. They'd land on a little platform outside the coop, the bell would ring, and the pigeon quartermaster opened the door, and in they'd go.

It was a beautiful morning, about like this; I can remember it well. The assistant flight officer, Lieutenant Commander Griffin, said to the pigeon quartermaster, "Let them all go." The pigeon quartermaster demurred a little. But the commander said, "Go ahead, let them all go."

So the pigeon quartermaster opened the coop and let all the pigeons out at once. They took off just like that, heading for Norfolk. They had been trained while the ship was in the Norfolk Navy Yard. They go back to a locality--they don't go back to a coop--and the coop can be anywhere. But what they do is go back to a locality.

While we were in the navy yard, after we were commissioned and before we went to shake down, the pigeon quartermaster would put the pigeons in a cage and put them on railway express and send them to Richmond or somewhere where the expressman would let them go, and they'd all come back to Norfolk.

So all at once, we had no pigeons on the Langley. Pretty soon we got a dispatch from the Navy Yard Norfolk. I don't know how they knew they were ours. They said, "Your pigeons are all back here. We haven't got any appropriation for pigeon feed."

We put the pigeon quartermaster in a plane and flew him down to Norfolk. They were all roosting in the crane where we'd been fitting out. After dark, he climbed up in the crane and picked them up. You can do that after dark. He took them over to the Naval Air Station Norfolk. That's the last we ever saw of pigeons on the Langley. So they made the pigeon coop into the executive officer's cabin, a very nice one incidentally.

Anyway, the Lexington and Saratoga had been laid down as battle cruisers. They were in the battle cruiser program. There were nice compartments up on the main deck, which was the deck below the flight deck, that were assigned as pigeon lofts, and one in each ship--big compartments.

One of the things that we did--I had hardly more than reported when we saw those. They'd make fine berthing compartments. So we got the pigeon lofts deleted from the plans of the Lexington and Saratoga and made them into berthing compartments. That's a little absurd, but that was one of the things we did.

Q: It brings up another point though. At what point did aircraft start carrying wireless?

Admiral Pride: The flying boats had them all through World War I. I don't know, and yet it's quite an historical event. But it was before World War I when they were experimenting on that.

Q: The planes that you were flying did have wireless then?

Admiral Pride: Yes. The ones we used for flying off the battleships had radio in them to transmit our spots back the first year. Of course, we didn't get voice on the

Pride #2 -59-

planes until after World War I. The first voice I encountered in a plane was in some sets they sent down to us in Cuba, to use to spot. But they weren't very satisfactory. We still sent our spots back by dot and dash, after we did a little trial.

Q: So you not only had to be a good pilot, you had to be a radioman also.

Admiral Pride: You had to be your own radio operator, yes.

Q: What other things did you apply to the Saratoga and the Lexington that you learned on the Langley?

Admiral Pride: We had learned considerable about what sort of repair work you would do on a ship. We rearranged the shops and their equipment accordingly. We had found out what spares you needed to carry. For instance, you were going to have a fairly high incidence of landing gear failures, much more so than in landing aircraft ashore. We were able to readjust our supply list and the supply storage in the ship.

We had some very firm ideas about the handling of the aviation gasoline, the handling of the aircraft on deck, and the securing of the aircraft when they were on the ship.

Q: Were the aircraft kept on deck all the time, or were they stowed below?

Admiral Pride: We stowed them below or kept them on deck, according to the next operation. We liked to get as many of them below as possible, of course, to get them out of the weather.

We learned quite a lot about the handling of aircraft on a ship.

Q: After they were commissioned, what happened to you?

Admiral Pride: I stayed in the Lexington for a cruise. Then I was ordered back to the roads to work up the gear for the Ranger, which came after the Lexington and Saratoga.

Q: What did you do on the Lexington on the cruise? Were you flying?

Admiral Pride: Yes, I was flight deck officer. In those days, the ship's officers did considerable flying, too. We had the squadrons aboard. When the squadrons would be ashore, say, at North Island if we were on the West Coast, the ship's officers did a great deal of flying on and off the ship. There was still quite a lot of developmental and experimental work to be done.

We weren't at all satisfied with a lot of the things we were doing. There was room for much more rapid operation than we had. We were always trying out things. We were not happy with the deck lighting system for night work. So we redesigned the deck lights.

Q: Did you take off and land at night?

Admiral Pride: Yes.

The signaling, coaching the pilots as they came in for their landings--we weren't completely satisfied with it. But we didn't have any very good ideas as to how to improve it, but we tried various schemes. The business of using arm signals to show whether the pilot was high or low or fast or slow came about in an interesting way. We were at anchor in the York River when the ship was being shaken down.

Q: Which ship was this?

Admiral Pride: The <u>Langley</u>. The executive officer was Commander Kenneth Whiting, who had been largely responsible for our having a carrier. He was in the netting, just below the flight deck level where the personnel goes while aircraft are landing. He used to stand in the netting all the way aft on the port side. That was a good place to see what's going on.

We had one pilot who had not landed on the deck before, but had had a lot of training and practice ashore.

Let me go back a bit. Up to that moment, it never occurred to any of us that anybody could know any more about handling the airplane than the fellow that was flying in it. It was a very parochial point of view, but it was one that all pilots had at that time.

This chap came in, and apparently he was very reluctant to actually set his plane down. He kept coming in high, and then he'd give her the gun before he quite got to the deck, and go around again. This had happened several times. Whiting jumped up on the deck and grabbed the white hats from two bluejackets that were there, and he held them up to indicate that this character was too high. Then he put them down. He coached the fellow in, and that seemed like a good idea.

So from then on, an officer was stationed aft there with flags to signal whether the plane was high or low or coming in too fast or too slow.

Q: So it was really a spur of the moment...

Admiral Pride: Yes, it was a stroke of genius by Whiting. Out of that has grown the present very sophisticated electrical signaling system.

Q: Where did you go while you were on the Lexington? Where did you cruise?

Admiral Pride: We went into commission at Quincy in December. We did some taking on of stores and fitting out and so forth in Boston; we went in dry dock in Boston.

We were keen rivals with the Saratoga. We and the Saratoga went into commission less than a month apart, as I remember.* Then there was much rivalry as to who should have the first landing aboard.

---

*The USS Saratoga (CV-3) was commissioned 16 November 1927 and the USS Lexington (CV-2) on 14 December 1927.

The Lexington was to go right from the shipyard at Quincy into dry dock in Boston. The Saratoga, a day or two after that, was to go down the Delaware River and have her trials. I suspect this, but didn't know it, but the Saratoga figured they'd beat us out by having a landing on board while they were going down the Delaware River.

Our skipper, Captain Marshall, instead of going straight to South Boston, detoured out into Massachusetts Bay just long enough for me to land aboard.* Then he went up into the dry dock in South Boston. So we figured we'd done pretty well. We made our landing before the Saratoga. It was very childish, but those things, of course, are part of life.

Q: Competition makes it interesting.

Admiral Pride: Until the Lexington was sunk, we were always in keen rivalry.

Just as in battleships—when I was in the Arizona we were keen rivals of the Pennsylvania.

---
*Pride made the first takeoff and landing on the Lexington in a UO-1 on 5 January 1928. Commander Marc A. Mitscher, USN, made the first takeoff and landing on the Saratoga in a UO-1 on 11 January 1928. Captain Albert W. Marshall, USN, was the first commanding officer of the Lexington.

Q: That's the way it always is.

Admiral Pride: Sure, that's human as can be, and it's very fortunate it's that way.

For one thing in the carrier development, it sped up our operations like everything, because we were always trying to land aircraft or take them off more rapidly than the other ship. It was a powerful incentive.

After that, we went down to Norfolk and took some squadrons aboard. Then we went to Newport, Rhode Island, to get our torpedoes. Then we went around to the West Coast.

Q: Through the Panama Canal?

Admiral Pride: Yes, which was disastrous for the Panama Canal, because the ships had these huge overhangs. The pilots had never handled ships like that before. I remember when we went through, in going in the Gatun Locks, they didn't get the ship straightened up enough. As we went into the locks, the overhang would strike those huge concrete lamp posts they had, and over they'd go. The first one everyone regarded as quite a disaster and was so sorry. But as the second one went down, the crew all had a great interest. As each succeeding one went down, the crew all had a great interest which provoked a certain amount of irritation, as far as the canal people were concerned.

Q: Were you sailing alone, or did the Saratoga come with you?

Admiral Pride: No, we went around together.

Q: What was the purpose of the cruise?

Admiral Pride: The Navy Department had decided to have both ships on the West Coast; the major threat was felt to be in the Pacific at that time. It took a long time after that to develop; this was in '28 that we went around.

Q: So these ships were no longer considered experimental? You were operational?

Admiral Pride: We were operational.
    When we got to the West Coast, we went in for post-

trial repairs in San Francisco. Then the Lexington was selected to make the high-speed run to Hawaii, in which we broke all transoceanic records.* Then we came back and did regular squadron operations.

Q: While this was going on, what was happening in other countries in their development of aircraft carriers, or how did that affect you?

Admiral Pride: The French were building the Bearn. I think they had started the Bearn at this time.

The British had the Ark Royal, I believe. They were coming right along; they were right about abreast of us. Their gear was quite different than ours, most of it. Some of it, in later years, we've adopted, such as their steam catapult.

We were operating more airplanes faster in our ships. We were singularly fortunate, in a way, I suppose, in having the large hulls of the big battle cruiser hulls of the Lexington and Saratoga.

---

*On 12 June 1928, the Lexington anchored in Lahaina Roads at the end of a speed run from San Pedro, California, to Honolulu, Hawaii, that broke all existing records for the distance. Elapsed time was 72 hours and 34 minutes.

Q: How much were you affected by what they were doing? Were you aware of what they were doing?

Admiral Pride: Yes. We weren't telling each other officially much of anything. In fact, we were trying to keep it secret from each other. But an awful lot of that information does get out.

For instance, when we were in the <u>Langley</u> and anchored in Bar Harbor, there was a British cruiser in there at the same time. We could see them taking pictures of our operations whenever we were flying.

No, we were trying to be very secretive about this. I don't think we were especially successful.

Q: What about the Japanese? Did you know what they were doing?

Admiral Pride: The <u>Lexington</u> and <u>Saratoga</u> were considered in the 1922 Disarmament Treaty. At that time it was decided not to complete the six battle cruisers, in fact not to complete any of them. Then it was agreed that the <u>Lexington</u> and <u>Saratoga</u> could be completed as aircraft carriers, provided they kept within a tonnage limit of, I think, 36,000 tons.

The Japanese were all for this, because they had some big ships under way.* I think, as aircraft carriers they had them planned. They said that they would agree to our completing ships as aircraft carriers, if they could keep their program going. I think that's the case, but that ought to be checked. It's so long ago.

Q: Did you ever get involved in the politics of all this?

Admiral Pride: Oh, no, I was too far down the line. Commander Whiting used to take me to the meetings of the General Board in the Navy Department to talk about these things.

At that time, the General Board, which is no longer in existence, was composed of about seven, as I recall, very senior officers. They were charged, by the Secretary, with advising on the characteristics of ships and on any other question that he figured he wanted some very mature advice on.

I can remember one meeting very well, in which--as

---

*The Japanese Kaga and Akagi began construction as a battleship and battle cruiser respectively. Under the provisions of the Washington Treaty, they were completed during the 1920s as aircraft carriers and served in that capacity until they were both sunk during the Battle of Midway in June 1942.

all ships do--it was getting heavier as it was being built, that is beyond the design and intentions as these two ships were. This was recognized in the General Board.

The question was, "Would this violate our treaty? And if so, how was anybody going to know about it?" The General Board said, "No. If these ships exceed their tonnage, it will be violating this agreement, and it simply cannot happen." In this particular meeting, I can remember, the discussion was largely around what items should be left out of the ships in order to keep them within the treaty limitations.

Q: What did you feel about that at the time?

Admiral Pride: I felt it was exactly right. I admired these people for being so honest about this thing. Because the other parties to the treaty were never going to be able to measure the ships actually. It could have been sneaked, but there was no dissent at all. They said, "Here is the case; what are we going to do about it?" They agreed that they'd just have to leave out some items.

One item that seemed important at the time, and in the operation of the ships in the years that they were in commission that would have used a great deal, I guess--the original plans as carriers provided some diesel plants in them to provide power when we were at anchor. It took out quite a bit of tonnage to leave these out.

They had 16 firerooms, and they were pretty big plants. It would have helped a lot. It would have been economical and helped in our overhaul work in port, if we could have shut the whole steam plant down. But the diesels were left out.

Actually I was very thankful, if I can jump way ahead, that I knew about this. Many years later, when I was executive officer of the Saratoga, we ran out to Hawaii as soon as Pearl Harbor happened. We were entering San Diego when that occurred. We'd come down from overhaul in Bremerton. We immediately took on fuel and supplies and headed for Hawaii the next morning. We unexpectedly had to refuel some destroyers that met us on the way, which drew us down very low. It was touch and go as to whether we'd have enough fuel to get to Hawaii. We figured we'd just about make it.

We got off the harbor entrance there. We were about to come in, and we got a signal from the beach that Japanese submarines were operating off the island, right off the entrance, and for us to haul off and make an approach later. We did, but, gee whiz, I began to worry like everything. And the chief engineer began to worry like everything.

Although we had residual fuel in the ship, it was very highly subdivided. It was in lots of compartments, and you only had a few gallons or barrels in each compartment, but you couldn't get them. So as we came in later, the engineer called up and said, "I'm going to run out of fuel."

I said, "Oh, no, you're not. You've got two tanks of diesel fuel that we have never used. You can use that." And he said he could.

So we came into Pearl, came into the channel, on this old diesel fuel that had been in the ship for years. Just as we got our first lines out, I looked up, and out came the white smoke. We couldn't have gone another mile.

Q: That was very fortunate.

Did anything significant happen while you were on the West Coast on the *Lexington*?

Admiral Pride: We made a high-speed run.

A very significant thing happened. It doesn't sound so to you, I'm sure, but I mentioned it before. In the <u>Saratoga</u> was a naval constructor named L. C. Stevens.* We'd been closely associated in this arresting business for a long while. He said, "Let's take the fore-and-aft wires out." Which was done; they've never been put back, and it saved an awful lot of aircraft. It was a very significant change in our operations.

These things would get tangled up in the fore-and-aft wires, and you had to hold off aircraft from landing several minutes while you'd get them out. They would break landing gear, break propellers.

I wished afterwards that I had had the imagination to get rid of these abominations.

Q: That's funny, because that never even occurred to me that they would be there.

Admiral Pride: I think that's like other things. You buy something, and then you feel that you have to justify it. This was called the B gear and was bought from the British. Then you felt that you had to justify your investment.

---
*Lieutenant Commander Leslie C. Stevens, Construction Corps USN.

Q: Did you stay on the West Coast until you left the Lexington?

Admiral Pride: Yes, I was detached from the ship out there. She stayed there, of course, except for a cruise back here, in connection with fleet maneuvers.

I had been thinking about this hydraulic gear. The Norden gear was another technical disadvantage, in that these winches on each end were independent of the thing. If you hooked a wire, and you were off center, the thing--just through physics--had to steer you toward the side of the ship, and you'd go overboard. Which I knew, because I'd seen planes go over. It was a terrible thing. So I felt that the design had to be changed to obviate that difficulty.

So I was ordered back to Hampton Roads when I left the Lexington in '29.

Q: Did you ask for that duty?

Admiral Pride: No.

Q: Did the Navy know that you had had some plans?

Admiral Pride: Yes, I was pretty well identified with this business by that time. The Navy wasn't as big as it is now, and individuals were identified with particular interests, probably more so than they are today.

No, I didn't ask for it. In fact, I was a little worried, because I was a line officer, and I felt that I was getting somewhat overspecialized in engineering.

The AED, aeronautical engineering duty designation, didn't come in until I left the Lexington. Then it was suggested that I join that group. I said no, because I wanted to retain the prerogative of command. So I remained a line officer.

I was ordered back there, and once I got back there, I really got down to work on it and developed the hydraulic gear and some other deck fittings.

Q: Can you tell me a little about your experimental work when you were in Norfolk?

Admiral Pride: The experimental division there, not only were we working on arresting gear but we had miscellaneous tasks and experiments.

Q: Was this a fairly large station at this time?

Admiral Pride: The Norfolk station was, but my own group was small. I usually had only a civilian engineer and probably three or four pilots in a little machine shop. A machinist, a warrant machinist, a couple of chief machinist's mates--probably in the whole crew there were 50 or 60 people.

Q: Were there other than aeronautical experiments going on there?

Admiral Pride: No, I can't remember anything that wasn't aeronautical. The aeronautical ones were very diversified. For one thing, because the water was there, the sea, we got all the seaplanes and flying boats for their rough-water trials. I ran all of those.

We'd get experiments like a radio ranging thing. Some Frenchman sold it to the Navy. It looked much like the omnirange now. It was way ahead of its time; it didn't work at all.

We had ordnance trials occasionally, the ones that were of interest to the Bureau of Aeronautics. All of those that were of interest to the Bureau of Ordnance went on at Dahlgren. Sometimes there'd be overlap, and we'd get the aeronautics part of it.

Q: Something occurs to me that I hadn't thought of before, that is when you brought up seaplanes and flying boats. Your experience is almost totally in carrier planes.

Admiral Pride: In World War I, I started out in flying boats. We were designated first as heavier-than-air pilots if we weren't lighter than air. Then I was designated as multi-engine flying boat pilot. Although actually in France, I only flew single engine ones. We didn't have any multi-engine ones there.

Q: Were pilots divided between carrier aircraft and land aircraft versus seaplanes?

Admiral Pride: You had to be qualified for it. No, you didn't have any formal designation.

Q: What I mean is, once you became proficient in one, did

you tend to stay in that particular area? Would there be sort of two different groups?

Admiral Pride: Yes, you would. The big-boat pilots, as they were called--the big multi-engine pilots stayed pretty much in the field. I never heard of a fighter pilot going back to flying boats, for instance. There was no reason legally why he shouldn't. Until they got rid of the flying boats, that was pretty much of the case.

When I was ComAirPac, I doubt if the flying boat squadrons had very many pilots in them that had been fighter pilots on the carriers.*

There was a certain amount of thought, in later years especially, of rotating all pilots through all these types. I was against it myself, because I thought that pilots had a hard enough time trying to keep abreast of, not only the piloting business, the aircraft business, but if they were going to eventually command carriers and carrier forces in fleets, they'd better darn sight learn how to be sailors, too, and keep their hand in steering the boats as well as aircraft.

Q: I can see the reason for that.

---

*Admiral Pride was Commander Air Force Pacific Fleet from 1956 to 1959.

Admiral Pride: It seems to me that the business of--to use the slang phrase--steering the boats is a highly technical operation, especially men-of-war. You'd better get all the time in that you can, rather than spend any of it qualifying in various types of aircraft.

Q: We're getting away a little bit from the experimental work. That's my fault; I asked the question.

Admiral Pride: One of the experiments--we spent quite a bit of time in developing a deck lighting system. There again, the original lights in the ships' decks for landing were simply deadlights with electric light shining up through, which gave you a very poor sense of depth. You didn't have very much of an idea how far away they were; there was a certain glare around them.

We went back through the literature and found that the French had found, in World War I when they had to establish sort of little emergency landing fields for their planes returning at night, that if they just put lanterns out and the pilots looked directly at the source of light, they didn't do very well. But if they shaded the lantern so that the light was reflected from a board painted white, they had pretty good depth perception.

So we made the deck lights that involved the reflection. If I remember things, that's the only thing that I got a patent for. I didn't want a patent for it. Being a deck fixture, it came under the Bureau of Ships. To my astonishment, one day, I got an imposing looking document saying that I had been awarded patent number so-and-so for a deck light that was being assigned to the Navy, for which I was receiving one dollar. But I never got the dollar. I have the diploma somewhere, but I never got the dollar. I thought that if I got that check, I'd frame it.

There was urgent need for a deck fitting, to tie the aircraft down. Simple as it sounds, it isn't quite that simple, because it has to be flush with the deck obviously. There had to be an awful lot of them. They shouldn't form pockets that can retain fuel that can burn. So we developed the cross-deck channels with the hold-down fittings in the covers of these channels.

Q: Did you enjoy that work?

Admiral Pride: I loved it, sure, because I had a free hand.

Q: Did you have projects assigned to you?

Admiral Pride: Sometimes. We'd dream them up ourselves.

There was a desk in the bureau, of course, to which I made my weekly reports, or special reports on projects.*

They sent various ones, simple things like shock absorbers. And wheel brakes, I remember we had quite a lot of those when they were just getting started. In the olden days, there were no brakes on the wheels.

We had one that was a peculiar thing. Somebody thought we might be able to use them on carrier decks. I don't know why, but they told me to go ahead and try them out. I think they bought them from France. Instead of a wheel, it was a little caterpillar tread about five feet long; it went right on where the wheels go. Of course, it was pretty silly engineering-wise, because here was this belt that maybe you'd be landing on. In those days, it was much slower than now. Maybe you were landing at 65-70 miles an hour, and here was a tread that had to get up to that speed right now.

A wheel would scuff a little--you'd hear them when you'd land, you'd hear them squeak. That's quite different than having a mechanical tread that leads over a

---

*The bureau referred to here was the Bureau of Aeronautics.

couple of pulleys--one fore and one aft and some others in between. They'd have to start that whole mechanism going from nothing up to 60 or 70 miles an hour, right how. It didn't last long.

Q: Why was it developed?

Admiral Pride: I have no idea; it seemed completely illogical to me. I think the Frenchmen developed it probably, thinking it would do on soft ground, where a wheel would sink in and this caterpillar tread would not.

Then they sent us down a set of skis, saying, "Instead of landing on wheels on the ship's deck, if you land on skis you'll have enough drag. So try them out."

I tried those out. Of course, it was easier to try them out and show their fallacies than to go into an argument about it. It was very evident right away that you never knew precisely, within some fairly large range, where an airplane would touch the deck, for one thing. It might touch at the stern, or it might touch halfway up through the gear. When you wanted to land, where it was going to stop, you had no idea. Furthermore, the damn things, with all that drag without the axle, you went right over on your nose.

Q: Wasn't there danger of catching the cables?

Admiral Pride: This was to get rid of all the cables. Then, of course, if you did stop, then you had to handle the thing and push it out of the way. They had a lot of notions like that.

Q: What did you do your experiments on? Did you have an aircraft carrier there?

Admiral Pride: No. We started on a turntable that was only 100 feet in diameter. By the time I got back there from the tour of duty that started in '29, there had been built a dummy deck, which you could not rotate into the wind as you could the turntable, but it was built into the prevailing wind. It was several hundred feet long and a very good replica of the ship's deck, flush with the ground. It had the galleries underneath, on which you could mount the arresting gear and all that stuff.

Q: Were you able to make adjustments to it? You talked about putting in the fittings for it.

Admiral Pride: Yes, it had a wooden deck. When you

wanted to try out anything, it was easy to cut it out and put in the fixtures.

Q: How did the test of the autogiro come about?

Admiral Pride: It had been under development, and someone--it might have been me--suggested that we ought to test it aboard ship. So one fine day when the Langley was off Hampton Roads, I flew out to the ship and landed.* You had to be careful because the deck was so narrow, and there was also a problem when landing into a breeze. Unless you turned left immediately, the rotor would fly up and break a blade. So, as soon as it landed, I swung hard left and had to stop before going over the side.

Q: How did it differ from a helicopter?

Admiral Pride: In a helicopter, you've got power to the rotor, which wasn't true in the autogiro. Sometimes when the main engine goes out in a helicopter, it will autogiro to the ground. The autogiro could make a vertical landing

---

*On 23 September 1931, Lieutenant Pride piloted the Navy's first rotary-wing aircraft, the XOP-1 autogiro, in landings and takeoffs on the USS Langley (CV-1) while under way.

onto a carrier's deck, but it took off like a conventional plane.

Q: Did anything come of this development?

Admiral Pride: No, because it became obvious that a helicopter would be much more capable.

Q: Where did you go after your experimental duty?

Admiral Pride: Among other things, we were testing out the Navy's first dive-bomber that was built as such. It looked to me as though that was a pretty good field to get into. It had great promise if we did go to war. So I asked to be assigned to the first squadron of these dive-bombers. That technique had just been in the Navy a short while and obviously had great promise. So I was assigned to this dive-bomber squadron that was to go to the Langley, which was then in the Philippines. But when I got to San Diego, I think it was decided just about the time I got there to not commission this squadron, or maybe the Langley wasn't to go there just at this time or something. I've forgotten just why.

Anyway my orders had to be cancelled. I was ordered to command VF-3, a fighter squadron, again on the Langley, with Boeing F4B-4 aircraft, which were the nicest airplanes that we had at that time. I was delighted with this.

We did a lot of dive-bombing with the fighters. I had that squadron for two years. Both years were sort of frosting on the cake. We were the Navy squadron at the National Air Races.

Q: You competed in that?

Admiral Pride: We didn't race; we just put on demonstrations.

Q: I'm not familiar with dive-bombing techniques or problems. It was fairly new then.

Admiral Pride: Yes. The bombing was pretty inaccurate, especially if you were trying to hit a ship. Because a near-miss wasn't much good; you had to hit the ship.

It may have been Miles Browning who had this notion; I'm not sure.* That can be checked in the literature.

---

*Lieutenant Commander Miles R. Browning, USN, commanding officer, Fighting Squadron Three. Browning relieved Pride as commanding officer of VF-3.

Whoever it was had a stroke of genius. Of course, instead of aiming the bomb, you'd aim the airplane in a vertical dive. At first, you tried to push over. It's very, very hard to push over in a vertical dive and do it quickly, because the acceleration throws you out.

It was then decided that, instead of pushing over to do your dive--and in this it's highly important to be absolutely vertical--to roll over on your back first. You'd roll over on your back and then you pull the stick into your dive, just sitting in your seat that much more firmly, and you don't lose consciousness. The pullout, of course, you like to make it as low as you can, but that's limited by the acceleration you can stand at the bottom of the dive and that won't pull the airplane apart. The pilots black out usually at about six G. So that you had to judge your pullout so that you'd be out of your dive without exceeding six G.

Q: That must have been a very risky thing, testing, when you first began doing it.

Admiral Pride: It didn't seem to be particularly risky.

Q: For instance, somewhere along the line somebody had to determine that it was six G's.

Admiral Pride: Yes. That had been pretty well known for a long time, just in acrobatics and in testing aircraft. In demonstrations and tests you pulled them out to some predetermined gravity to see whether they are structurally strong enough. So that the pilot limitation has been known for a long while.

That was stepped up by using anti-G suits much later. Those came along after my experience in fighters. The suit is pumped up; it puts pressure on your body so that the blood doesn't all leave the brain. You can stand a higher G.

Q: Where was the Langley during this time while you were commanding VF-3?

Admiral Pride: Our home port was San Diego. We were the so-called "battle line carrier." We were usually with the battleships.

Q: During that period of time you were mostly training and cruising?

Admiral Pride: Oh, yes, we had many, many fleet exercises. In between exercises and cruises we'd base on San Diego and be doing our gunnery, training the pilots, and stuff like that.

Q: You were flying yourself at this time?

Admiral Pride: Yes, I was squadron commander.

Q: There's a general question I'd like to ask you. It has to do with the experimental work as well as your operational flying. What contacts did you have with companies that were developing aircraft?

Admiral Pride: A great deal. I knew all the head people on a personal, first-name basis.

Q: Did you trade findings?

Admiral Pride: Yes. They'd bring a plane to Norfolk. Well, they didn't bring it; we usually ferried it down ourselves. Some would arrive in crates. According to their contract, the demonstration flight had to be made by a company pilot. He demonstrated that the thing could be recovered from certain attitudes. He dived and was required to pull a certain amount of G's to see if it was structurally sound. That usually took only one or two flights, if it was satisfactory.

Then a Navy pilot took it over and did lots of things--fired the guns, bombing, and everything. He felt the controls to see if the thing was a good flying machine.

Inevitably, there would be bugs in the first demonstration. The company people would be right there as you came down and say, "What do you think of it?" And you told them what you thought was wrong or what you thought was right. They would always have a crew there to try and fix it up right away.

Q: Had you reached the point where you were asking for aircraft designed for aircraft carriers?

Admiral Pride: Yes, we were. As the planes grew heavier and faster, it was no longer a question of just hanging a hook on the tail somewhere. The loads in the tailhook were getting very high. They were running about three

G's; for a 12,000-pound plane, there would be a 36,000-pound load in the trailing hook with peaks that would run sometimes as high as six G's. So you had to absorb these loads into the structure of the airplane. These loads began to have to be worked into the design of the aircraft. Also the landing gear loads--the wheels and axles had to be beefed up and stresses carried up through into the airplane structure.

So we couldn't just take the same aircraft that the Air Corps, for instance, was using and hang a hook on it and land it on the aircraft carrier. If we did, it wasn't going to work. The plane had to be designed for this work.

Q: So by the time you commanded your squadron, you were flying aircraft that were carrier aircraft?

Admiral Pride: Yes, the F4B-4 was very distinctly a carrier aircraft. The Army had a version of it, but it didn't have to have a hook built in on the landing gear the same as ours. They had a weight advantage on us for some years because of that. They could make their structure that much lighter. They would have been foolish to carry this weight around.

Pride #2 -92-

I guess I'm getting into modern politics now, but the same aircraft was not compatible for the Air Force and Navy, as was found on the F-111.*

Q: There was quite a bit of screaming and yelling over that.

Admiral Pride: This was evident to a lot of us. This was not hindsight, because we discussed this almost every time some of us would get together. It was fairly evident for quite a while before the aircraft ever flew that it was never going to be flown by the Navy. It just didn't fit into our environment.

Q: I can see where the difference would be there. Where did you go after your duty on the Langley?

Admiral Pride: I left the Langley and came back to the Navy Department as the Navy working member of the Aeronautical Board, which is something that you've probably never heard of.

---
*During the 1960s, when Robert S. McNamara was Secretary of Defense, he tried to develop the F-111 as a common Air Force-Navy plane. After a good deal of protest on the part of the Navy, the Navy version was finally cancelled.

It was felt by somebody, about 1919, that the President needed an agency to advise him on military aeronautical matters. So this thing called the Aeronautical Board was set up, in which the members were the Chief of the Bureau of Aeronautics and the Chief of the Army Air Corps. Then there was a member, not an aviator, from the Navy, and another, not an aviator, from the Army. There may have been one or two more, I'm not sure. Each service had a working member, who kept the office going. There was a lot of work done. One of our main projects was standard specifications for aircraft.

Q: You were the working member?

Admiral Pride: I was the Navy's working member.

Q: What rank were you then?

Admiral Pride: I was a commander. We were legally an agency of the White House. But practically we worked in the Navy Department; we had our office there. Of course, it was pretty much of a service operation.

I think it was a fine thing. The Aeronautical Board,

long before I went to it, had made the decision, for instance, that the Air Corps would go ahead with the development of liquid-cooled engines, and the Navy would go ahead with the development of air-cooled engines. That was a very fine thing. It concentrated engineering attention and skill in each service on one line of endeavor and saved taxpayers an awful lot of money. Otherwise, we would have had both types of engines going in both services. The thing would have been all spread out and very extravagantly.

Q: Did you in the Aeronautical Board assign priorities to various developmental work?

Admiral Pride: No, that was pretty much assigned to us. We had a lot of odd jobs too. As I said, one of our principal concerns was the standardizing of specifications, and that went all the way from paint to rivets to complete engines.

Then another thing was if some company wished to sell anything aeronautical or ship anything aeronautical abroad--either material, equipment, drawings, or design information--by law it has to be licensed. The license is issued by the State Department. The State Department relies, of course, on the recommendations it gets from the services. At that time, and as long as the Aeronautical Board existed, the Aeronautical Board prepared those license recommendations upon which the White House and State Department acted.

I loved that work, because it got you pretty well acquainted with a lot of foreigners. I was sorry when it was decided to do away with the Aeronautical Board, because I felt it was a very useful instrument of government. But several years ago it was decided to discontinue it.

Q: Do your remember exactly when that was?

Admiral Pride: No, I don't. I was long gone. I left there in April of '41 to go to be the executive officer of the Saratoga.

Q: You talked about standardizing specifications. Did you do the actual work, or did you have a staff?

Admiral Pride: I had some engineers and draftsman to do

it. The Army chap and myself would decide on it. We'd get people in from the naval aircraft factory at Philadelphia and from the Army material command at Wright Field. Then we'd decide on what the specification for parachute silk would be, how many threads to an inch and all that sort of thing. Then the engineers and draftsmen would go ahead and draw up the formal specifications for this material. Then that would go to other departments for their comments. Then it would become a government specification.

The whole series of AN standards were developed, as long as it lasted, in the Aeronautical Board.*

---
*AN--Army-Navy.

Pride #3 -97-

Interview Number 3 with Admiral Alfred Melville Pride,
U.S. (Navy Retired)

Place: Admiral Pride's home in Arlington, Virginia

Date: 18 April 1970

Subject: Biography

Interviewer: Peter Spectre

Q: Admiral, the last time we talked, we talked about your tour of duty on the USS Langley, which you left in June 1934. Could you tell me what happened to you after that?

Admiral Pride: I was ordered to command the Flight Test Section, which was then at the Naval Air Station Anacostia. I remained there until the autumn of '34. I cracked up in the Potomac River and went into the hospital for several months but was kept on as the flight test officer. Upon my return from the hospital, I resumed that work and after a while was transferred to the fighter desk in the Bureau of Aeronautics.

Q: What was involved in the accident that you had?

Admiral Pride: I was making high-speed runs at low altitude over a measured course in the Potomac River near Indian Head. The main fuel line broke, just forward of the fire wall. The gasoline came into the cockpit and started to burn.

I was too low to use my parachute. It was a seaplane.* I attempted to land it. As I got down, just barely off the water, I couldn't hold my breath any longer. And I couldn't breathe, because I would have breathed in the flames. So I thought she would probably land; the pontoon was almost on the water. As I say, I couldn't hold my breath any longer, and I had to get out of the flames. My ankles were burned, as well as my face. I reared up and out and let go of the stick. Instead of landing, she tore the pontoon; it tripped and cracked the plane up. I had it trimmed nose-heavy anyway for the high-speed runs. You had to do that to balance it.

Q: So how did you get out?

Admiral Pride: I was in the water; fortunately, I wasn't pinned in. The engine had come back and smashed my leg. Somebody came rowing out from the ordnance station at Indian Head and took me and the mechanic out of the water.

---
*The crash occurred on 4 September 1934. Pride was flying an X03U-6.

Pride #3   -99-

The mechanic, fortunately, was not hurt. But I had been pretty well stove-up and burned.

Q: What kind of testing did you do at Anacostia?

Admiral Pride: We tested all the new aircraft that the Navy bought, and put them through the routine flight tests.

Q: Was this before they were bought, or after they were bought?

Admiral Pride: They had all been bought. Before a plane is delivered, a new type, a company pilot demonstrates it. He puts it through various maneuvers and attitudes to see if the thing is structurally safe and that it's all right aerodynamically. For instance, it might go into a tailspin and the characteristics of the ship be such that you couldn't get it out of the spin. When he's gone through these demonstration flights, it's then turned over to the Navy pilots of the Flight Test Section, now at Patuxent, who put it through a very extensive series of tests to measure performance and stability and to determine in broad terms its service suitability.*

Q: Did you reject planes?

Admiral Pride: Oh, yes.

Q: What was your average?

Admiral Pride: I don't believe I could say. Practically every airplane that came through would have to have some corrections made in it.

In those days, oftentimes before placing a contract for a production order, preliminary contracts had been let, probably with three companies. We would select the one that was the best of the three for production. The other two were not turned back to the company; they'd been bought on contract. Very few planes were just sent back to a company because they were completely unsuitable; the contracts weren't written that way. But most every plane had to have various corrections made in it, and they still do.

---
*Now the Naval Air Test Center, Patuxent River, Maryland.

Q: Did you test planes by type? In other words, if a new type of plane was being sold or proposed to be sold to the Navy, did you test just the initial plane from that type, or did you test every single plane?

Admiral Pride: No, the initial plane. Quite frequently, especially in the transports and training fields, companies would send their own planes down for us to fly them and make a quick evaluation--in other words trying to sell them to the Navy, getting our reactions. That happened quite often.

Q: What you were really dealing with was prototypes?

Admiral Pride: Yes, that's right.

Q: It sounds hazardous, especially since you yourself had an accident. What was the casualty rate among test pilots?

Admiral Pride: It was pretty high. I'd hate to give a figure, but I wouldn't say there were very many of us left. Of course, I'm pretty old now. We had enough casualties all right.

Pride #3 -102-

Q: What other type of work did you do there? Was it mostly operational work?

Admiral Pride: I was the officer in charge of testing. As such, I was legally on duty with the Board of Inspection and Survey--which by law is charged with passing on all the ships and airplanes that the Navy buys--and running the trials.

So there had to be very long reports written on all these tests, to see not only that it was a suitable airplane but to satisfy the requirements of the contracts, which were very detailed.

Q: The planes that you tested--did the Navy request a design for a particular need? Or were these airplanes that were more or less invented by a company and sent to the Navy to see if they could use them?

Admiral Pride: The process ordinarily went about like this: the operating forces would indicate the need for a type of aircraft, or sometimes these needs would be foreseen within the Navy Department, probably more often than in the fleet itself. The Navy Department would be aware of the state of the art and realize potentialities maybe that people out in the fleet were not acquainted with. On the other hand, people in the fleet would come up against requirements in the operations which would indicate that a certain type of aircraft was desired or necessary.

The Bureau of Aeronautics, which was charged by law at that time with the design and procurement of aircraft for the Navy, would draw up a set of specifications. In some cases, those specifications would be nothing much more than an envelope of design, saying for instance that we require an aircraft that's small enough to go down an elevator on an aircraft carrier. In the case of a fighter, it's got to carry certain armament and have a certain envelope of performance. It's got to fly to competitive altitudes and competitive speeds.

The engineers in the bureau, who were very competent, would take this envelope of design, as you might call it, and examine the state of the art at that time, or what was projected for the next several years, and what power plants would probably be available. You almost never designed around an existing power plant, because they were being developed rapidly. You took a chance usually that you would have a certain power plant, and so much power available by the time the plane was built.

The specifications then would begin to narrow down. It must use a power plant of such characteristics, and certain items will be furnished by the government. That would restrict the thing a little bit more. That would be especially so in armament, power plants, and navigation and radio equipment.

So that these specifications became quite specific, and they would be put out to the industry, maybe go out to as many as ten or a dozen different contractors. Anybody that wanted to, if he were a responsible contractor, could submit a design for proposal. From the specifications, he would draw a preliminary design, give its characteristics that he would be prepared to guarantee. This would be called a design contest. On a given date, these designs would be opened. Then there would be probably months of evaluation of them. Usually about three of the most promising would then be given contracts to build planes. We would get these three planes and evaluate them competitively.

Q: That's what you did at Anacostia then, you'd test

three planes of a particular type to compare one against the other?

Admiral Pride: Yes. The production plane having been selected, we would get the first production plane that came through and put it through a very rigorous series of tests to see that it met the contract requirements and it met the service requirements.

Q: During the period of time you were there, what were some of the planes that you tested?

Admiral Pride: The one that I was injured in was an observation plane. I've forgotten the designation of it now. It was a Vought aircraft.

We had quite a number of fighters come through about that time: two or three Grumman planes, and some Brewsters, single and two-seaters. We had Curtiss observation planes, and a Curtiss amphibian. We had two or three flying boats come through, Martin, Douglas, and Consolidated, I think.

Q: When you first started flying you flew in seaplanes,

and then switched almost entirely to fighter type aircraft. So you were back in seaplanes again.

Admiral Pride: That's right.

Q: Was there ever any plane that you wouldn't fly--that it was delivered and you looked at it before you even took it up in the air?

Admiral Pride: Oh, no, because they'd all been demonstrated. Their initial flights had probably been made at the company's plant. You knew they could fly; in fact, that's how they got there.

Of course, I had done a whole lot of this work at Norfolk, when I had the experimental section there. We tested all the seaplanes and flying boats for their rough water tests. Also, we landed them on the dummy deck, as I think I have said before. And we flew them at night, because we had an array of lighting similar to the deck lighting of a carrier, to see how they would be and if they were suitable for carrier operations.

Although we conducted the flight tests out of Anacostia, we took all the planes over to Chincoteague.

That is, we flew them out over the ocean out around Chincoteague for their gunnery tests. We went to Dahlgren for some of the ordnance work down there. We worked around various places. Our base was Anacostia.

Q: You were in the hospital after your injury. You got out of the hospital, and then what?

Admiral Pride: I went right back to testing.

Q: How did you feel about it? Were you gun-shy from your accident?

Admiral Pride: No, not at all. That was my job, and it was something I had always liked. I enjoyed very much flight test work.

Q: What did your wife have to say about your participation in it?

Admiral Pride: Nothing at all. As I say, that was our life. I had been on experimental stuff practically all of my career, flying off the turrets and all that sort of thing. She didn't like it. No wife likes it very much, but she never mentioned any fear.

Q: What was your next assignment after Anacostia?

Admiral Pride: I went to head the fighter desk in the Bureau of Aeronautics.

Q: Was this an assignment that you requested or what?

Admiral Pride: No, I was ordered over to it. The desk became vacant, and I was ordered to fill it.

I liked that too, because it gave me a chance to be in on the writing of specifications for aircraft. Also, with the class desk system that was then in operation in the Bureau of Aeronautics, all the reports of fighter operations from the fleet would come through that desk. Everything that had to do with fighters, for instance, came to that desk and then went on to maintenance or other offices in the bureau. So that you had your finger very much on the situation. It was attractive to me also to be in on the formulation of specifications for new aircraft.

Q: Did you use that position to put into effect any problems that you might have seen before you reached the desks--in other words, in what you'd seen in Anacostia?

Admiral Pride: Oh, yes, and in the fleet. That certainly influenced your work at the desk.

Q: What types of things do you recall that you believed in most that you tried to push in that particular period of time?

Admiral Pride: Well, of course, one of the things I suppose that every flight desk officer tries to do is keep weight down.

Q: Weight of aircraft?

Admiral Pride: Yes, especially in fighters. You felt that a pound of structure that wasn't required or that wasn't absolutely essential was a pound of bullets you couldn't carry or gasoline that you couldn't carry. It was a constant effort to keep weight of aircraft down, structural weight especially.

In those days we were very much concerned, those of us who had worked on carriers, with the vision out of the plane for carrier landings especially.

As an ex-squadron commander, ease of maintenance was a very, very strong consideration.

These are very general, but they are things that were in your mind that you were fighting all the time.

Q: Did you encounter any opposition?

Admiral Pride: No, you just had to sell them. The bureau was just trying to turn out the best planes it could. Of course, different people would have different views of the importance of certain factors. Sometimes, you'd have to try and convince them that your point of view was a little more valid than theirs.

Q: What about your contacts with the other services during that time? Did you personally work with the Army?

Admiral Pride: Yes. When they would have new planes out at Wright Field, for instance, if they thought we might be interested they would invite us. And we'd invite them to take a look at ours. I've gone out to Dayton and flown their types on occasion.

Earlier, while I was at Anacostia, we were considering a Curtiss aircraft of some kind, a fighter, I think, that would be a Navy version of one that the Air Corps had then. They very kindly lent me one of theirs to run some trials on to see how we liked it. It was a very good plane, one of the best.

Q: While you were on the fighter desk, did you get a chance to get away and observe some actual operations?

Admiral Pride: Not out to the fleet, no. I didn't get out to the fleet at all while I was in that job. I was over in Anacostia a great deal. And I was at contractors' plants quite a bit. One of the things that they do, and this is still the case--before the airplane is actually built, the mock-up is built. Some of them are pretty elaborate. They look as though you could fly them. Others are pretty elementary.

One of the jobs of the desk officer was to go and view the mock-up during its construction, and when it was completed, he organized a mock-up board, which had armament and radio experts and all the different experts. They'd go out and criticize the mock-up and catch many things that the contractor's people had maybe overlooked, or more often simply hadn't realized were important. This would be especially so in the pilot's cockpit. That involved visiting the contractors' plants frequently.

Q: Did the contractors at that time, as they do now, hire retired people from the services or people who had been discharged?

Admiral Pride: Yes, usually one or two of them or maybe more. Most every plant you went to, you met somebody you'd known before.

Q: What happened after you did your tour in the fighter desk?

Admiral Pride: I went from there to be air officer of the Wright.

Q: Where was the Wright stationed?

Admiral Pride: She was in the Pacific. The Pacific Fleet was then called the Battle Force. The Wright was the flagship of the flying boat squadrons. The captain of the Wright was Captain Mitscher.* Rear Admiral King had his flag in the Wright.** While I was in her, he was relieved by Admiral Blakely.***

Q: Will you tell me something about the Wright, what type of ship she was?

Admiral Pride: The Wright had been built as a World War I cargo ship, or to be a transport. I think the Argonne was of that class. They were of wartime construction. She had a big hold aft that had been intended for a kite balloon, and it served very well for us to put seaplane spares and stores. We had accommodations for the crews of seaplane squadrons, which we tended. She actually tended these squadrons.

One summer we went to Alaska for instance. We had four squadrons up there and spent a good part of the

---
*Commander Marc A. Mitscher, USN
**Rear Admiral Ernest J. King, USN, Commander Aircraft Scouting Force, U.S. Fleet and Commander Patrol Wing One.
***Rear Admiral Charles A. Blakely, USN.

summer in Kodiak just to learn something about the operation of naval aircraft in that part of the world. Also to look over Kodiak and see whether it would be a suitable place for an air station in case we needed one up there.

D: Did the seaplanes land on the deck, or did they land alongside?

Admiral Pride: No. These were flying boats, the big fellows. The only time you ever brought one aboard was when something had to be repaired.

Q: So it wasn't really a carrier?

Admiral Pride: No, not a carrier. It was a seaplane tender. It also served as flagship for the flying boat squadrons of the scouting force.
Another time we went out to Johnston Island, for instance. We stopped in at Hawaii. And then went on out to Johnston Island and based there for a while. We wanted to see how you'd carry on operations if you had to in that part of the world. Also to evaluate Johnston Island as a possible site for an airfield.

Pride #3 -115-

Another time, along about New Year's, we took four squadrons and went down to Panama, over to Puerto Rico, and up to Norfolk and Newport, and back to San Diego operating on various fleet problems in all those places.

Q: Did you fly yourself?

Admiral Pride: Yes. We had one or two smaller planes attached to the ship, and as air officer that's all I had available to fly.

When Mitscher became commander of the patrol wings, then I was his operations officer. Then I could fly a lot. I was also his chief of staff. We traveled by air from place to place then, rather than by ship.

Q: What type of duties did that involve, as chief of staff?

Admiral Pride: You were executive officer of the outfit. We had a very small staff. The only people on it were the doctor, and the communications officer, and a supply officer, as I recall. Which meant that I had to write most of the operations orders myself. I was a very busy boy in those days, especially when we'd had one of these cruises, such as around to the East Coast.

Q: How many other ships were involved?

Admiral Pride: I think we had on that cruise, when we came around to the East Coast, about four tenders. There was the Sandpiper, the Teal, and I think one other.

Q: What was going on in the Navy at that time about fighter planes and aircraft carriers versus seaplanes?

Admiral Pride: There was no contention. In the setup that we had at that time, the various types had distinct functions or missions which did not overlap very much.

The flying boats were distinctly for long-range scouting for both services and air types and went to ranges that the carrier planes could not go, whereas the carrier planes were a striking force. As compared to the flying boats, they had very short range.

Q: Was there any feeling in the Navy at that time that the day would come when flying boats and seaplanes would be obsolete?

Admiral Pride: I don't think there was, to look at it quite honestly.

I think most of us felt that the flying boat would always be able to do a job that the carriers could not do. Of course, in those days we didn't envision the carrier force being as large as it is now. The battleship was still very much in the picture. The notion that carriers would dominate the Navy--some people had it, but it was pretty remote.

Q: That brings us around to a very general question, and that is what the Navy as a whole thought about the aviation side of the Navy. This would include a span of the ten years around the time we're talking about, in the Thirties.

Admiral Pride: I think very early in our conversation I cited the reception I had received on one of the battleships. The captain assured me that aviation had no place in the Navy. Of course, there had been a lot of change from that.

During the Thirties, it was well accepted that if you were going to fight a war in which the Navy was to be involved, you were going to use aviation.

Pride #3 -118-

There were the inevitable rivalries of funds probably. That is with the usual budgetary appropriation limits, just as it is today and as it will be forever. A dollar the other fellow gets is a dollar you don't get. So the high naval authorities had to decide where they'd put their funds.

Q: I want to ask you for an opinion. Who do you think were the best friends of naval aviation during this period of time in the Thirties?

Admiral Pride: Of course, I can never say too much about Kenneth Whiting. And Admiral Moffett, of course, who had been Chief of Bureau of Aeronautics.* He had been killed before this time; he was killed in one of the dirigibles. But he had been a great influence, although he had not been an aviator before he came to the bureau.

In the early days there was Captain Chambers, who had great influence.** Then in the Thirties we had various

---
*Rear Admiral William A. Moffett, USN, Chief of the Bureau of Aeronautics from its establishment on 26 July 1921 until his death on 4 April 1933 in the crash of the airship Akron (ZRS-4).
**Captain Washington I. Chambers, USN, Director of Naval Aviation, 1910-1913.

Assistant Secretaries for Air who were quite influential. There was Dave Ingalls for one that I think of particularly.*

Q: Was there anybody who was a thorn in your side?

Admiral Pride: No, I can't think of anyone. I'm not weaseling on this; I honestly can't.

We were all enthusiastic, of course, and probably irritated a lot of people with our enthusiasm. Along in the Thirties, everybody took a very balanced view, it seemed to me. After all, the backbone of the Navy was still the battleship, and our operations were built around the assumption that it probably always would be.

Q: Even among the aviators?

Admiral Pride: Yes.

Q: What was the next assignment that you had after you left the <u>Wright</u>?

---

*David S. Ingalls, Assistant Secretary of the Navy for Air.

Admiral Pride: After I had been the chief of staff for Mitscher, I came ashore and came to the Navy Department as the Navy's working member on the Aeronautical Board.

Q: This is what we discussed in our second interview. Why don't we go on to the next thing after that period of time.

Admiral Pride: From the Aeronautical Board I went to be executive officer of the old Saratoga.

Q: Where was that ship based?

Admiral Pride: I joined her in the Navy Yard, Puget Sound. We worked in the fleet and the fleet exercises until Pearl Harbor.

Q: You had been on the Saratoga before.

Admiral Pride: I was in the Lexington. I was attached to the Saratoga for fitting out, when she was being built, for a short time. Then I was transferred to fit out the Lexington. That was back in 1926.

Q: You had never really served on the Saratoga?

Admiral Pride: No, not after she was finished. It was pretty easy, because the two ships were identical. I knew the ship, having spent between the two of them something over a year fitting out. So it was very simple to go aboard and to know the workings of the ship and how she was laid out.

Q: As the executive officer, this was really a line officer's duty. So that you were now handling ships rather than aircraft.

Admiral Pride: Both. After all, the ship ran its aircraft. When they were embarked, they were in the ship's organization.

Q: As far as the shiphandling goes, how was the transition for you?

Admiral Pride: I had had a good background in that when I was back in battleships as a junior officer and in the Langley. As a ship's officer I was the senior watch officer in the Lexington when I served in the Lexington from '27 until '29. So I had pounded pitch an awful lot.

Q: Is there any real difference between handling an aircraft carrier or a cruiser or a battleship?

Admiral Pride: There's a whole lot of difference between handling a big carrier and a cruiser. When I had the Belleau Wood, I had a cruiser hull under me. With all the power in her, it was a very maneuverable hull. Whereas a big carrier has an awful lot of inertia. If you want to stop and back, she doesn't stop and back anywhere near as quickly as a cruiser does. If the wind catches her when you're trying to make a dock and she starts to move, it's a whole lot harder to stop her. She's just a big, heavy ship. Of course, the battleships were, too.

It's comparable to handling a big, heavy automobile against a very light sport car.

Q: You were in the Saratoga just prior to our entrance into the war and immediately after. Can you tell me what was happening to you during this period of time, and what the Saratoga was doing?

Admiral Pride: I joined her in April of '41. We had gone for a little overhaul at Puget Sound just before the war started.

Then we came down to San Diego. We were entering San Diego on the morning that Pearl Harbor was attacked. So we were ordered to fuel up and get on out to Pearl as quick as we could to see what we could do out there. We did; we got under way the next morning and headed for Pearl. After going to Pearl, we refueled and took stores and got organized into a task force. We headed out to relieve Wake. Before we got there, we were told that relief for Wake was no longer possible. We then took a squadron of Marines to Midway instead.

Then we went out on another trip and managed to get torpedoed. We were torpedoed on the night of the 11th of January and came back into Pearl for repairs. We were repaired sufficiently to get us back to Puget Sound, where the ship was put back into shape. Then we came down to San Diego, and I was detached.

Q: What were the events that surrounded your being torpedoed?

Admiral Pride: We were cruising in a force. It was after

dark, I suppose about 8:00 o'clock in the evening. I had gone below to have my dinner. We were hit right smack amidships on the port side by what the fragments--some of them came up on deck--indicated was a 21-inch Japanese torpedo. I always had the impression, especially by the shape of the hole and the extent of the damage, that we might have been hit by two, but the board decided not-- that one had done it. It did a lot of damage. It took out three of our firerooms and ruptured a whole lot of tanks. It did a lot of damage to the ship.

Just about the time we got hit, a signal had come across from a cruiser screening us for that that they had seen two torpedoes go by headed for us. By that time, we knew it.

I was ordered back to the Navy Department, to the Office of Procurement and Material, which had just been set up. They wanted an aviator in there with some engineering knowledge. I had a fairly general knowledge of aviation, so I was ordered to that.

Q: Did you want to go?

Admiral Pride: No, of course not. It was strictly a desk

job. Things were happening elsewhere.

It was a rather new office. There seemed to be a lot of people that were fussing around with the paperwork of contracts and so forth. It wasn't attractive to me.

After a very few months there, Admiral Towers, who was Chief of Bureau of Aeronautics, shifted me over to the Bureau of Aeronautics where I had sort of a nondescript job for a little while.* Then I was ordered to put the Belleau Wood in commission.

Q: Where was the Belleau Wood being built?

Admiral Pride: New York Shipbuilding at Camden, New Jersey.

It took me back to my old stomping ground. I'd been there with the Saratoga when she was being built.

Q: What stage of construction was she in then?

Admiral Pride: I went to her in the late autumn. She

---
 *Rear Admiral John H. Towers, USN, Chief of the Bureau of Aeronautics from June 1939 to October 1942.

went into commission in March.* So she was in her final stages of construction.

Q: What was the ship like? Was it built to be a carrier?

Admiral Pride: No. There were to be nine cruisers of the Cleveland class. It was essential to get flight decks out, into the Pacific especially. The quickest way to do it was to take these ships, several of which were already under construction and the others were coming right along, and make them into light carriers. The Belleau Wood was the third of that class to be so changed.

Q: Was it handicapped because of the change?

Admiral Pride: The only handicap about it was its small size. As a ship, it was a delight to operate. It was terribly hot below decks, about 120 degrees down in the living compartments when we were all buttoned up at battle stations sometimes. They were uncomfortable ships,

---

*The light carrier Belleau Wood (CVL-24) was commissioned 31 March 1943. When her keel was laid on 11 August 1941, she was intended to become the light cruiser New Haven (CL-76).

because everything was very cramped. When you took a cruiser hull and tried to put on squadron personnel and the aircraft, as well as the people to run the ship, they were terribly cramped.

But just from a shiphandler's point of view they were a dream to operate. They were very handy little ships. For instance, if we were cruising in a large task force, we could take over the fighter patrol, which you had to keep up all the time, without tying up one of the big ship's flight decks. We were available to send off on all sorts of side missions that you wouldn't want to devote the main force of the fleet to. Such as when we went down to occupy Howland Island and a couple of islands down there.

Q: How many planes did you have on board?

Admiral Pride: About 36, as I recall.

Q: And you were the commanding officer?

Admiral Pride: Yes.

Q: Where did you go after your left the shipyard?

Admiral Pride: We came out of the shipyard into our trial runs, which we made down the Delaware River, and they were very perfunctory. Then to shake down, we went down to Trinidad. We came back to Norfolk for our post-trial repairs. Then we went to Panama and from Panama across to Hawaii, where we fell in with the fleet.

Q: Can you tell me something about the various operations that you were involved in with the Belleau Wood?

Admiral Pride: One of the first ones was we had a little force and went down and occupied Howland and Baker Islands. We were in, it seemed to me, practically every operation that the fleet had while I had the ship. Because they were short of flight decks and short of air forces. Although they'd alternate the numbers of the fleets, we'd come back and replenish and then just go out with the other one.

Q: You have a list of the various operations that you did engage in. Would you elaborate on it a little for me?

Admiral Pride: We were in the occupation of Baker and Howland Islands. That was simply that two light carriers, the Princeton and ourself, were sent down with a landing force. It didn't amount to much of an operation. There was no real opposition. The planes from the Belleau Wood shot down one Betty, I think. I don't know whether anybody else had any action or not. That was just a sort of a pleasant cruise. That was in September of '43.

Then in November of '43, we had a similar operation at Makin Island. That was rather uneventful. Then, of course, on Tarawa and Wake and Kwajalein, we had a lot of action. I lost some of my pilots in some of those affrays. But the ship was never damaged. We saw our first kamikaze up at Saipan. We had been to Tarawa, Saipan, Truk, Palau, Yap, and Woleai. Then I was relieved and sent ashore at Pearl to command the naval air bases in that naval district and got my promotion.

Q: You mentioned that you met your first kamikaze. Where was that?

Admiral Pride: Yes, that was off Saipan, as I remember. We didn't know anything about kamikazes then. But this Betty came in low, just off the water, and headed right for us. Everybody was shooting at him, but nobody was stopping him. He came right through the screen and headed right for my amidships. Of course, we were shooting at him as best we could. He caught fire; his port engine started to burn just before he got to us. I don't know what happened, but maybe the pilot was killed or something. When I was sure we were going to catch it right amidships, I had started the ship turning so to catch him as much end-on as I could, but he was still coming right down. He zoomed down right over my bridge. Pieces of him were falling out, and into the water on the other side and blew up.

I'm thoroughly convinced, from my later very extensive experiences with kamikazes up at Okinawa, that he was trying to run into me. Thank goodness, he did not.

Q: That must have been frightening to see.

Admiral Pride: Exciting. Not so frightening, you just sort of, well--the big idea, of course, was to try to shoot him down before he got there.

Q: What else sticks out in your mind? You'd been through a whole series of invasions and operations. There must be some things here that you remember more than others that might be of interest.

Admiral Pride: I think one of the most trying ordeals I ever went through was when we were on our way to Kwajalein. The elevators on those ships were slung on cables. The cables for some reason or other--there was a pretty heavy sea running--jumped the sheaves. There was my forward elevator out of action down, which meant that I couldn't use the flight deck. Here was business coming up, and we were out of action.

Q: Did you have planes in the air at that time?

Admiral Pride: No, fortunately not. It happened in the early evening, as I recall. By golly, the crew turned to. It looked hopeless at first. Here was this big heavy elevator--it was cocked up like that, but they jacked her up. We got about halfway through that job, when I got the report that my condensers were salting up. Both casualties were corrected, and we got into the business all right and did our job. I was an awful worried man for a while.

Q: Were you the only carrier with this force?

Admiral Pride: No, it was a big force. I didn't want to be out of it, so ignominiously especially.

Q: What other things do you remember?

Admiral Pride: Another thing that still puzzles me no end--you remember the casualties, I suppose, more than anything else. You had plenty of room for casualties. You had an awful lot of people that had never been to sea before. You had a very high-performing engineering plant. We were still having lots of trouble with radar. And these little ships were awfully lively; you had to be very careful about your maneuvering so you could get your deck as steady as you could for your planes to operate and land, especially. So I suppose I remember casualties more than anything else.

I was just leaving Pearl one day to go out; fortunately it was just for some exercises. We had this refresher work for the squadrons. We were just clearing the channel when the engine room called up and said, "We're salting up very badly on the condensers." I didn't

Pride #3 -133-

do a thing but turn around and report that I was coming in and asked for a tug, because I didn't know whether I was going to get in or not under my own power.

I've often wondered about that, because all of our piping was in good condition. We couldn't see where the salt water had come from, until we finally discovered in the after part of the ship there was a place where the fresh water and salt water systems could be cross-connected. We had some sort of emergency, I don't know what. But that was supposed to be blanked off with a blank flange, so that it couldn't happen accidentally. And the flange had been removed. I've often wondered how that could have happened.

Q: Did this happen to you often?

Admiral Pride: Only those two times. The other time there was a little leak in the condenser or something like that. So we quickly discovered what it was and corrected it.

We were very fortunate. We never caught a kamikaze in the ship. But I turned it over to Jack Perry down at Majuro.* He hadn't had her very long before he caught a

---
*Captain John Perry, USN.

kamikaze. It burned out the whole aft part of the ship and killed about 400 people.

My only serious casualty, I suppose, that actually cost lives on board was one night a plane came into the barrier on landing, cracked up, and caught fire. That burned up a gun crew. We were very fortunate that there was not more extensive damage.

Q: At this time you were a captain?

Admiral Pride: Yes. When I went ashore, I got my commission. It was the day before I left the ship, it came in over the radio that I'd been promoted.

Q: What was your new assignment?

Admiral Pride: That was when I went to command the naval air bases of Hawaii.

Q: What did that involve?

Admiral Pride: The general supervision of all the air stations in the central Pacific. There was a lot of construction work going on. Most of it had to do with that and the acquisition of bombing ranges, target ranges, and operation of such things.

Q: Did you enjoy that assignment?

Admiral Pride: Not any more than you ever enjoy being on the beach when you figure there's some business going on at sea--no, not particularly. It was a pleasant way to live, but professionally it was not enjoyable at all.

Q: What were some of the difficulties that you encountered?

Admiral Pride: I don't think there was anything difficult at all. Probably trying to decide priorities was the most, if there were any difficulties. Because there wasn't much concern as to what things cost. The question was, "How do you allocate what can be shipped from the continent?" The supply of building material and such was limited, of course, and of fuel, by the shipping from the continent. Your biggest question was, "How do I allocate what lumber, concrete, and fuel oil and so forth I can get?"

Q: How big was your staff to help you with it?

Admiral Pride: I don't remember, I suppose 30 or 40 people.

Q: Did you spend much time touring the stations?

Admiral Pride: Most all the time on the road. There wasn't very much to be done back at the headquarters that the staff couldn't do. But you felt that you had to be on the go. There's always something that doesn't show up on the correspondence. The only remedy for that is to actually go and take a look yourself.

Q: Were you in that position until the end of the war?

Admiral Pride: No. I escaped from that in about ten months and went out to take over the air support in the amphibious force. Kelly Turner was Commander Amphibious Force and I went to go with him, to take over the air support.* I took that over at Okinawa. I spent about a month makee-learn, trying to find out what it was about,

---
*Vice Admiral Richmond Kelly Turner, USN, Commander Amphibious Forces Pacific.

and then was able to take over when we went to Okinawa.

Q: What did you do?

Admiral Pride: Directed the air operations at Okinawa. The arrangement was that the Navy kept the command agreement, which had been drawn up, which is always drawn up before those big operations--was that the Navy should retain control until the "situation became stabilized."

Admiral Spruance was in overall command, and Admiral Kelly Turner was commander of the amphibious force, which did the actual operation.* In the <u>Eldorado</u>, which was his flagship, we had three headquarters and three staffs: his and my own and General Buckner, who was to take over for the Army when the situation became stabilized.** It was decided that the situation had become stable about the middle of May or the 1st of June (we went ashore April 1st, as I recall) and General Buckner went ashore.

We went down to Manila. During the Okinawa thing, as I recall, we had planned something known as "Black Hawk," which contemplated landing on the mainland of Asia, at

---
*Admiral Raymond A. Spruance, USN, Commander Fifth Fleet.
**Lieutenant General Simon B. Buckner, USA, Commanding General, Expeditionary Troops (Task Force 56).

Shantung, I think it was. That was cancelled and in Manila we planned the invasion of Japan. It involved controlling not only Navy aircraft but Marine aircraft and Army aircraft also. So you had to have a cross section on your staff. I chose as my chief of staff Colonel Megee.* He reminds me, whenever I see him, that was probably the only time in which a Marine has been chief of staff for a Navy character.

Q: All during this period of time, especially after you became rear admiral, what role did you play in planning the strategy and the tactics that were to follow?

Admiral Pride: It was my job to prepare the air plan for the invasion of Japan. At first, I worked on Black Hawk, which was cancelled fortunately. It would have been a vast mistake. I had this Marine as my chief of staff. I had also detailed to me an Air Force brigadier, because they, of course, were going to be in on it in a big way. We spent our time preparing the air plan for the invasion.

That was an interesting thing to me. From

---

*Colonel Vernon E. Megee, USMC, chief of staff to Commander Air Support Control Units, Amphibious Forces Pacific.

Washington, from the Combined Chiefs we would get the overall plan. Then we would work up the details. The first overall plan called for us to land on Honshu, up above the Bay of Tokyo. This is largely conjecture, but I think it's probably so. We knew we were going to be in awfully bad trouble because of the terrain. Afterwards, when I was in the Seventh Fleet, I went up there to look it over, and we would have been.* Because we had fine beaches to land on, but when you left these beaches you had about a mile or two of rice paddies before you came to hard ground. We would have been slaughtered.

When the thing was laid out, the Japs had a lot of people over in Manchuria. They began to be moved down to Japan, which indicated that they had anticipated what we were going to do. And their movements indicated that they had it pretty well figured out where we were going to land. In all those amphibious operations the character of the beach is awfully important. This was one of the places that made a beautiful landing beach, but--so our plan was then shifted by Washington to have a slant at Kagoshima. So we had to change our plans all around,

---

*This refers to Admiral Pride's tour of duty as Commander Seventh Fleet from 1953 to 1955.

because this was an entirely different terrain. It would have been a terribly ghastly operation, I think, because apparently the Japanese began to figure that, because they put some fairly heavy artillery up on the headlands that are on either side of the Bay of Kagoshima.

Also they were going to be operating on interior lines for the first time. Heretofore we'd go to Okinawa or Guam or somewhere, and they would have had to come across the ocean after we began to dominate the situation. But here we'd be working on them there. They had all interior lines; you couldn't get between them and where they were coming from.

Also our radar, which we depended on so heavily, was going to be impaired, because it's hilly. They could come down low with their aircraft and be into our ships before we had any radar warning. So it was with considerable relief that I realized that they were not going to have to go to Kagoshima.

Q: Did you know beforehand about the bombing?

Admiral Pride: Not a bit, no. It was a complete surprise to me. I had been up to see Curt LeMay just a couple of weeks before that, to talk about the Air Force part in the proposed landing on Japan.* He gave me sort of a rundown on what their capabilities were and how he suggested they take part. As I was about to leave he said, "Do you know anything about Big Boy?"

I said, "No." I just thought he meant a great big bomb of some kind and shoved off. I know he would not have told me if I had said, "What is it?" He was not in any position where he could tell me. But it never dawned on me; I didn't have any idea that we had an atom bomb. Living right with him, I'm pretty sure that Admiral Turner didn't know anything about it.

Q: It was a very well kept secret.

Admiral Pride: It was wonderfully kept.

Q: Could you tell me a little bit more, Admiral, about the last portion of the war that you were involved in? You were planning for the invasion of Japan.

Admiral Pride: That was just a matter of sitting in the

---
*Major General Curtis E. LeMay, U.S. Army, Commanding General, 21st Bomber Command.

ship down in Manila and trying to work up the plans. As always, of course, one of the most difficult parts was communications. Everybody wanted a frequency, and there were a limited number of frequencies which your equipment could handle. I recollect that as being one of the most difficult parts.

I don't know if this is very diplomatic, but working the heavy bombers in--Curt LeMay's outfit--to the best advantage required a certain amount of consideration. The Army was always uneasy about having heavy bombers in any operation for fear they'd bomb their own troops. The dive-bombers, of course, they liked, because they could be relatively accurate. But they felt that if the heavy bombers tried to bomb the front lines, their inaccuracy might bomb their own troops. So you always had to reconcile the Army with the heavy bombers, because it was an awful lot of capability you couldn't throw away.

I enjoyed it very much. I enjoyed it more when I found out we didn't have to do it.

Q: When did you know that you wouldn't have to go through with it?

Admiral Pride: After the second bomb was dropped. There

was great almost reluctance to believe that the first bomb actually happened or had the effect that it had. It was just too good to be true. That's probably a very poor adjective. But you'd had several years, and this was going to go on and on, and all at once here was its termination.

You knew it couldn't go on much longer because of the reports that we were getting. They were getting so awfully low on aircraft fuel, for instance. Their logistics were running low. The number of planes they were losing, and the number they could possibly have indicated that they must be getting short of aircraft. So it couldn't go on forever, but still when it actually happened, at first it was hard to realize that it had actually happened.

Q: What did you think about this? What were your feelings at the time when you heard about the first bombing and the second?

Admiral Pride: Great relief that the whole thing was over, I suppose. I don't think it amounted to much more than that. We like to read, "Do we feel guilty?" and that sort of thing. No, I don't think so.

I think this was probably pretty well summed up, when I was in the Seventh Fleet and made a call the first time at Nagasaki. I went ashore to make my call on either the governor or the mayor. We were just chatting. I'd been wandering around through the devastated area, and the people were either just paying no attention to me or just nodding. There was no animosity evident. I remarked on this to the mayor or governor, whichever he was. I said, "I'm astonished that there seems to be no animosity in the streets toward me."

He said, "No, if we had had the bomb, we'd have done it to you."

Q: I'm sure that's true.

When the war ended, what became of you? Did you go to the surrender in Tokyo Bay?

Admiral Pride: No, I wasn't there. I wasn't in the hierarchy. I came back to Pearl. I came back to start to demobilize the amphibious force there. Of course, that was pretty routine.

The Office of Procurement, which didn't have any legal basis to start with, had been officially recognized by Congress. On the 16th of January '46, the Congress authorized the establishment of the Office of Naval Material, which came out of the Office of Procurement, with Admiral Moreell in charge.* They'd been working on it for some time, to get it officially established as the Office of Naval Material. Admiral King had said, yes, he'd go along with this--he didn't say it to me, so this is hearsay--but they'd like to have one aviator over there.**

I guess he knew I was about due to come home. After all, I'd been away for a long while, for most of the war. So somebody, I don't know who, said, "Pride's it."

So I came as one of the four division heads of the Office of Naval Material. I found myself with very little to do. One of the things was that we had to get rid of wartime surplus. I didn't enjoy very much being in the junk business; it was far from being at sea. However, I was stuck with that until I could escape, which I did in a few months and went to sea again as Commander Carrier Division Six.

---

*Vice Admiral Ben Moreell, Civil Engineering Corps, USN.
**Fleet Admiral Ernest J. King, USN, Chief of Naval Operations.

Q: There's a question that seldom gets asked, and I'd like to ask it. When the war ended, was there any question in your mind that that was the end? You were certain that that definitely was the end of the war?

Admiral Pride: No, you wondered if there wouldn't be some sort of trickery. You felt that the other side could not maintain the war much longer, but it was very hard to realize that it was all over. You sort of wondered if there was going to be some sort of unanticipated flareup somewhere or other or that they'd pull something dastardly, even though they had the surrender signed. I think that was just reflex; it wasn't really figured out. But I think it was in lots of people's minds.

Q: Did you see it as the end of war in general?

Admiral Pride: No, not at all.

Admiral Turner is dead and so he can't deny this, and I don't know as he'd want to, because I think he should be rather proud of it. There was a meeting in Manila, to which I was assigned--either after the bombing or the surrender I can't recall--to consider where the line should be drawn in Korea and how far south should the Russian influence come. I'm pretty sure Admiral Turner, at that time, wrote a note to General MacArthur, who was on the beach there saying in effect, "Keep an eye on the Russians."*

There was no feeling that this was the end of war. I think for those of us especially before we got into the war who had read Churchill's The Ramparts We Watch and stuff like that, that this wasn't the end of war by a long shot.

Q: Your next assignment was Commander Carrier Division Six.

Admiral Pride: Yes. That was back in the Atlantic. Our home port was at Quonset. I had my flag in the Leyte, I think. I joined the ship at Quonset. Then we did some exercising. Then we went over to put in a cruise in the Mediterranean.

Q: What was the purpose of the cruise?

---
*General of the Army Douglas MacArthur, Supreme Allied Commander.

Admiral Pride: Every six months, the ships of the Sixth Fleet would rotate, and it was our turn to be the Sixth Fleet carrier division.

Q: How many ships were involved in your division?

Admiral Pride: I think we had only two carriers in the Mediterranean at that time. Then we had four cruisers, a whole slew of destroyers, and some submarines and tenders.

Q: Your flagship was a carrier?

Admiral Pride: Yes. The actual Commander of the Sixth Fleet had his flag in a cruiser, but he had a lot of quasi-diplomatic work to do, too. So he turned over the tactical control of the fleet to whatever senior officer happened to be afloat there, and I was it, which I enjoyed very much. I could steer boats around.

Q: What was the mission of the fleet?

Admiral Pride: The American presence in the Mediterranean area, and showing the flag. Also we had various war plans for the support of our people ashore in the event of hostilities on the shore. It was a lot of conjecture, though we had to gear in with the Army's plans for its operations in the event of hostilities in Europe. There was some question as to what would happen. The Greek question was still interesting, and you always wondered what was going to go on in the Middle East.

Interview Number 4 with Admiral Alfred Melville Pride,
U.S. Navy (Retired)

Place: Admiral Pride's Home, Arlington, Virginia

Date: 12 January 1984

Subject: Biography

Interviewer: Paul Stillwell

Q: One thing that I am sort of curious about, just to start off on a general question, how were you accepted by fellow flag officers, in that virtually all the rest of them were Naval Academy graduates and you were not?

Admiral Pride: I was the first one that wasn't, in the line. Oh, perfectly. I never could see any distinction at all. I had been very fortunate, of course, in that I was quite young for my rank in comparison with others. I never could see the slightest difference in their attitude toward me than toward each other.

Q: Well, I'm sure you had established a service reputation by then, so they knew you were a competent officer.

Admiral Pride: Well, I hope so. I don't know. Of course, things like that, an awful lot depends on luck.

You happen to be there when the opportunities come along. I think your career is very largely a matter of just plain good fortune. You happen to be on this spot at the best time.

Q: Well, that works both ways, and in your case it turned out very fortunate.

Admiral Pride: Yes. I was fortunate.

Q: In these carrier divisions you commanded right after the war, you had commanded the Belleau Wood. How would you compare the ships themselves, the various classes--the Essex class and the Midway class?

Admiral Pride: Well, the Midway class was, of course, a bigger, more able ship in most every way. When I was over in the Sixth Fleet I had the, I think it was the Roosevelt, with me a good part of the time. Her additional capabilities were very good. That's a very difficult question to answer just offhand. The Midway class was bigger, later, and a better class in every respect, I'd say.

Q: Was there any difficulty operating formations with dissimilar types?

Admiral Pride: No. During the first part of World War II, when I was executive officer of the Saratoga, there was a certain difficulty there. There was difficulty there all right because of the difference in the Lexington and the Saratoga's characteristics, with the characteristics of later ships. The later ships had a much better turning radius, for instance, and better acceleration. But in operating the mixes between the Midway and the earlier ships, I never could see any trouble.

Q: Many senior officers look back and see their command of a single ship as the highlight of their careers. Did you feel any sense of loss when you no longer had a ship under your complete control?

Admiral Pride: Well, I think I'm pretty adaptable and adjusted pretty well to it. But I loved being the captain of the ship, of course. Anybody ought to. It was a pretty active command, and there was the satisfaction of putting her into commission and then taking her into action.

Q: Was there any sense of frustration then when you were a division commander, that you didn't have that same relationship with the crew?

Admiral Pride: No. No. I found my time pretty well occupied. No, I never felt that way. Those skippers have got their ships, but I've got the division.

Q: What sorts of things does a division commander do in having his time occupied?

Admiral Pride: Well, of course, when you're operating you're actually maneuvering the ships all the time and laying out programs, matters of, as you say, showing the flag, considering, "Well, the next port I'm going to be in is Piraeus, and what are the conditions there? What's their attitude toward the Americans right now?" You've always got disciplinary matters to review. Of course, your actual schedule comes to you from the Navy Department. So you know that you're going to be here on a certain day and somewhere else later on. But there are a lot of details that have to be considered.

Q: Are there any of your staff members that you particularly recall from that period?

Admiral Pride: Well, no. It always seemed to me I had a pretty competent staff. Of course, you had quite a bit to say in selecting your staff before you ever went to the job. You took people along with you that you felt could do the work. But no, I can't think of any people that I had on my staff that impressed me either as being outstanding or--they were all competent officers. No, I can't mention anyone.

Q: Did you have any involvement with CinCNELM? Admiral Conolly was in that job at the time.*

Admiral Pride: No, no, we didn't have any business with them at all.

Q: Do you recall any particular incidents of protocol or port visits in this ambassadorial role?

Admiral Pride.: Well, I don't know that I can

---
*Admiral Richard L. Conolly, USN, Commander in Chief U.S. Naval Forces Eastern Atlantic and Mediterranean.

remember any incidents. I know that I enjoyed very much becoming more familiar with the Turkish people and officers--their viewpoint. I was talking with one of their most senior officers one day, an Army officer. He had taken me up into their training area above the Bosporus there. And I said, "How are your troops distributed?

And he said, "Well, they're in three groups. We've got a group up on the frontier. "Then we've got a second group; they're back in training. And the third group is home on leave."

As we went up through their training area, I said, "You seem to be awfully short of vehicles." They didn't have many trucks.

He said, "Well, these people are the group that are going up onto the frontier. The people that are up there don't have any vehicles, because they're not going anywhere. They're just going to stay there."

I thought, well that's quite a remarkable change of pace from our very mobile forces.

Q: That was the period of the Truman Doctrine and containment of Communism. Did you see concern on the part of the Greeks and the Turks about the threat?

Admiral Pride: It seemed to me that the Greeks that I talked with seemed to be more concerned with their internal affairs. The Turks, though, seemed to be very aware of the Communist threat. To them it was an everyday thing and very real. They got along with surprisingly little.

Q: What about the Italians? Do you remember any relationships with them?

Admiral Pride: Yes. Of course, we used their ships in the NATO maneuvers when they got going and I visited them in Taranto, I guess it was, they were very top-heavy with flag officers. They had lots of them, but I wasn't terribly impressed.

Q: Did they feel any sense of embarrassment over their lack of achievement during the war?

Admiral Pride: No, no. I don't think that's part of the Italian temperament at all. They, of course, had really taken some pretty rough shots. Later on, when I was in the Bureau of Aeronautics here, I became very well acquainted with the British naval attache. He was a naval aviator and had taken part in the bombing raid at Taranto when they went in and did so much damage.* I was quite impressed by the way the Royal Navy had handled that whole thing. On the other hand, when we went down into Suda Bay and saw the poor old British cruiser--I think it was the York --that was sunk there, her upper works still awash, and realized that she'd been sunk by one of these little motor torpedo boats.** They had a net out, but this thing leaped right over the net and went in and hit the ship. They didn't do very well in that situation. But, of course, we didn't do very well at Pearl Harbor either.

Q: No. Did you get into Southern France at all?

Admiral Pride: Yes, we were in Cannes for a while, a little while, not very long. But I saw very little of the French Navy people, very little of them. No, I didn't see very much of the French. We used them some, but I

---

*An attack by British carrier aircraft on ships of the Italian fleet in the harbor at Taranto, conducted 11 November 1940. There were some parallels between the British attack and that by the Japanese at Pearl Harbor a year later.

**On 21 March 1941, the 8,250-ton British heavy cruiser York was torpedoed at Suda Bay, Crete, by an Italian motor torpedo boat. The ship was beached to avoid sinking but then was further damaged by air attack on 22 May 1941 and abandoned.

didn't have anything much in the way of a personal relationship with them.

Q: In general how were American Navymen received in these Mediterranean ports?

Admiral Pride: Most of them very well. I think that it was up in La Spezia that they had signs, "Americans, Go Home," or "Yankees, Go Home." But everywhere else we did all right.

Q: Well, the Italians had some pretty hotly contested elections during that period whether they would go Communist or not.

Admiral Pride: Yes. The only place that I actually saw signs of "Yankee, Go Home," was when we were in La Spezia up in Northern Italy. In Milan we seemed to be received perfectly all right, and, of course, we were all over Naples all the time anyway.

Q: Did the crews have the average number of disciplinary problems or more or less?

Admiral Pride: I think we had even less. That was a question that was frequently asked me. It seemed to me that both the Sixth Fleet and then the Seventh Fleet, when I was in the Seventh Fleet, we didn't seem to have much discipline difficulty. In fact, it was very good over in the Seventh Fleet. Of course, reading in the papers about these things like the drug business--we had none of that at all.

Q: More likely it was somebody that got drunk and took a poke at one of the civilians.

Admiral Pride: Oh, sure. I think in Naples they did throw a couple of our men into their jail there. One of the incidents in Naples came New Year's, when they throw their crockery out of the windows and off the tops of buildings into the streets. I instructed the shore patrol, "You'd better wear hard helmets." And then the chief of police of Naples sent out word, would I please rescind that order, because they would look so belligerent. I said, "I'll rescind it. I'll tell them to all stay under cover all the time." Which I did; nobody got hurt.

Q: The period that you were operating over there with the carrier division was the time after the great demobilization and also a period of retrenchment. Did that cause you any problems?

Admiral Pride: I cannot remember any specific problems. But I think we were feeling the lack of reenlistments. We were all feeling that. But we were able to operate our planes all the time. The ships kept going. I could not say there was some condition that was the result of that. But it was very much in our minds all the time that we had a situation there that we hoped could be rectified. We went into Norfolk, and the recruiters for the companies were in business right outside the gate. A man got paid off and we would hope that he would reenlist, but they'd hire him away. I think we felt that, but I can't think of any specific instances that were the result of it.

Q: Did you notice any drop-off in the performance of the air groups as a result?

Admiral Pride: No, I can't say I did. It seemed to me they performed awfully well. No, we didn't have to lay up more than the normal number of aircraft for maintenance or anything like that.

Q: Did you have to cannibalize people from other ships at all in order to make deployments?

Admiral Pride: We didn't during my time, but later when I got out in the Pacific we were keeping some people out there deployed much too long. That, of course, was beginning to show up in our lack of reenlistments. But in my time in the Sixth Fleet I couldn't see any of that going on. Well, I don't think we had as long deployments in the Sixth Fleet as we did in the Seventh. I don't think so.

Q: When it came time for you to move from there to the Bureau of Aeronautics, was the fact that you had aeronautical engineering education a factor in that assignment?

Admiral Pride: Oh, I imagine so. After all, I had my postgraduate in aeronautical engineering, and I had quite a bit of material experience. I had had the test division, flight testing, and the testing in the development of gear at Norfolk for the carriers. So I had a pretty good material background. And, I suppose that undoubtedly had its influence. And my scanty education before I came in the Navy had been in engineering school, too. But I'd been very fortunate in my assignments. It will probably sound a little absurd, but I think one of the most valuable tours which I ever had was in being ordered to a battleship in 1919, or whenever it was. That battleship duty turned out to be invaluable, especially when in the later years I came to have my own ship. My duty as the executive officer on the old Saratoga was useful also. So that I not only was fortunate in having had the aviation experience, both operating and material, but I had quite a bit of shipboard. I'd come right up through the ranks in shipboard experience, which turned out to be very fortunate, as I say, later on in discussing carrier affairs from a shipboard point of view with people over in the Bureau of Ships, Bureau of Ordnance.

Q: It's interesting what all goes into making a qualified flag officer. At the time you're doing it, you have no idea what benefits will come later.

Admiral Pride: Oh, no, you don't. But all of these tours of duty, it seemed to me, were sort of accidental. The reason I went to battleships was that when we came back from abroad in World War I, the Navy very kindly ordered us to the stations nearest our homes. My home was just outside of Boston, so I was ordered to the Naval Air Station at Chatham, Massachusetts. After I had been there a while, we had a very fine man who was killed later, Nathan B. Chase, as our skipper.* Chase found that he was going to go down to take a course to fly land planes so that we would have somebody that could fly off of turrets. I said, "Gee, that sounds interesting." So I applied for that and was accepted. It was the Army Air Corps then. They put us through their regular course as though we'd never seen an airplane before. But then we became what was called rather grandiosely the Atlantic Fleet Ship Plane Division. We were the people to fly off the turrets. So that gave me my battleship duty, first on the Arizona and then on the Nevada, I think.

Q: Did you stand shipboard watches as well?

Admiral Pride: You bet your life. They made us stand all night watches, because we had to fly in the daytime. I

---
*Lieutenant Commander Nathan B. Chase, USN, naval aviator number 37, was killed in 1925 in an air collision while exercising his squadron in fighter tactics. Chase Field at Beeville, Texas, was named in his honor in 1943.

didn't appreciate that distinction. Yes, and those battleship watches did me an awful lot of good in years later.

Q: In what respect?

Admiral Pride: Oh, just reading signals and keeping station.

Q: You were a deck watch officer, officer of the deck?

Admiral Pride: Yes. Started in as junior.

Q: There was a great concern then for precision of maneuvering. Did you experience that?

Admiral Pride: Oh, yes, you bet your life! Well, our standard distance is 500 yards, and you've got some good-sized battleship there, and at 500 yards you can't be very much off station. And just the old battleship routine was well worth having under your belt.

Q: In one of your earlier interviews you indicated that aviators weren't all that welcome with the ship's company.

Admiral Pride: They weren't welcome at all. No, no.

Q: Were there specific ways in which you were made to feel unwelcome?

Admiral Pride: Oh, sure. I was in the gunnery department, and there it was quite obvious that they regarded us as quite superfluous to the Navy. In fact, I guess maybe it was when I reported in to the Arizona, I remember I called on the skipper, making my call on the skipper and he assured me that aviation had no place in the Navy except, I think I mentioned this before, possibly in the kite balloons that the battleships had.

Q: Well, it must have seemed quite an irony to you then a generation later when the aviators took over the Navy.

Admiral Pride: Yes, yes. Well, to look at it, it was very understandable. After all, we got more pay than they did. Flight pay was an irritation to them. And they would have been less than human if they had not resented it.

Q: Well, I think this daytime flying and nighttime watches might have been their revenge on you.

Admiral Pride: Oh, I think it was a little bit of that involved.

Q: Did you have any problems getting enough sleep then?

Admiral Pride: Oh, no. After all, the watch was only four hours long. You made out all right. And you didn't fly every day anyway. You had quite a bit of work to do on the little old airplanes, though, to keep them going. They were quite temperamental.

Q: Well, aviation was a very hazardous business at that time. Did you think about that aspect of it?

Admiral Pride: Oh, sure. Yes, you thought about it and figured, "Well, that's what I'm getting paid for."

Q: It's remarkable that you have survived that era, because many of your contemporaries died in crashes--from the old <u>Langley</u> on.

Admiral Pride: Yes, I was pretty lucky. I got pretty well stove up, but I survived. There again, just plain luck had so much to do with it. When I had the flight test business over here, one of them didn't test out very well, and I got pretty well scratched up and broken up. My burns came out pretty well, though my hands and face are all scarred. My left leg wouldn't grow together. It had a compound fracture down here. They let me go back to duty with a brace on it. They put a splice in the bone. We had, I guess it was probably one of the only two or three OX3U-6s that we were buying. I had to bring it in over by St. Elizabeth's, down the gully there because of the wind, which gave me a very short distance to land this thing. I pressed down awfully hard on the pedals, it busted the graft in the leg. I'd been in the hospital for six months with it, and they stuck me in for another spell and decided to cut the leg off. And, by golly, I was scheduled for the operation the next morning and a brand-new doctor Willcutts came to be chief of surgery.* They were taking him around to show him the cases and explained mine. He'd made quite a name for himself in combating

---
*Commander Morton D. Willcutts, Medical Corps, USN, later vice admiral.

infectious wounds. He said, "Well, let me go to work on it for a while." So he opened my leg up and gave me a lot of treatment and kept my leg. Well, it's crooked, but it kept me on active duty. Now, if Willcutts had been a day later, I'd have been retired. It was just luck as far as I'm concerned. I had nothing to do with it.

Q: Well, it's little things like that that make a big difference.

Admiral Pride: What happened was the gasoline line parted. I was making high-speed runs. We had at that time a couple of markers on the shore of the Potomac, and to calibrate the airspeed meter we'd take time as we passed these marks. I was making a high-speed run in a plane that I think was a Vought, which was a floatplane.* You had to trim her all the way forward, nose down, to have her trimmed properly for high speed. You had to roll the stabilizers all the way down. Well, the main gasoline line broke. There was a fitting in it that carried away, and I was probably only about 50 feet off the water. All at once, the gasoline came back into the cockpit and

---
*Admiral Pride's flight log indicates that the crash took place on 4 September 1934, when he was flying a Vought XO3U-6.

started to burn. I had had an old friend who had suffered very badly from having inhaled flames. So I didn't want to do that. So I reared back up, put my head up out of the flames, and then my hands began to burn, and I thought she'd land herself. But she was rigged nose down. When she touched the water, she tripped and went over and that drove the engine back in on my legs. Fortunately, the fire went out. But it was all due to a little brass fitting about three quarters of an inch in diameter, a threaded fitting and it broke and flooded the cockpit with gasoline.*

Q: Was that the closest brush with disaster of your whole career?

Admiral Pride: Well, I had another one when I was stationed at Chatham. I was flying an old H-boat up in the Connecticut River, up above Springfield somewhere. We were recruiting. Along about July of 1919, word came to let all the duration people that wanted to to get out. We had a crew there of about 300 people. The

---

*Admiral Pride also discussed this crash at the beginning of interview number three.

next day we had less than 100. But we also got orders to take two or three of these old flying boats and go out all around New England recruiting. I was doing that. And we didn't bother with physical examinations. We would get some kid in and sign him up. Anything to get a body back on that station. On the way down the previous day, for some reason or other, I suppose I put the plane in the bank and had been correcting a bump or something. I'd found that I had no left aileron. It was as though somebody had put a lock on it. But I could keep the thing level enough so that I went around and landed on the water. I went all over the control system, and I could find nothing wrong. But the next day I was up above Springfield, above the Connecticut River, and I turned around to make my turn to come back down the river, and to my horror, when got I banked up she wouldn't come back. I just couldn't turn the wheel at all. So she banked higher and went into the river. That time, I didn't get hurt. Fortunately, I had my hard helmet on. On those planes your--there was a Liberty motor right back here, and the crank made a dent in my helmet. If I hadn't had the crash helmet on, I'm sure it would have killed me. But, other than that I was just shook up a little. But I think I was closer to passing out on that one than I was on the one down here, although this one put me in the hospital for about 13 months.

Q: When you took over as the Chief of the Bureau of Aeronautics, what were the main things that the chief devoted himself to?

Admiral Pride: Well, it was very clearly laid out in <u>Navy Regulations.</u> He was charged with the procurement and maintenance of aircraft. That's fundamentally it. Of course, those days the chief of bureau did not report to the Chief of Naval Operations. That law went into effect when I had been in the bureau, I think, about two or three years. You were an agent directly of the Secretary of the Navy. The Secretary of the Navy made out your fitness report. You were also charged with the maintenance and operation, of course, of the naval aviation shore establishment, not the operational stations but the shops and things like that. For the maintenance I think the phrase is maintenance and repair of aircraft, something like that. But also, as I say, you had to make all the aviation appearances in Congress for anything in aviation except personnel. You had to defend the naval aviation budget. That took most of your time. What with supplementary appropriations--of which there are many, which most people don't realize--I guess I was on the Hill at least once a week all the time I was in bureau.

Q: Were there any noteworthy appearances before Congress that you recall?

Admiral Pride: No. I rather enjoyed it there. Of course, some of the time you had to sort of match wits with some of the interrogators. You grew to recognize who was likely to be most favorable to you. Occasionally, somebody would come along who was decidedly not. I used to love my questionings by Vinson. He knew more about the Navy than most any naval officer did. I remember when I took over one of the things that was on the desk to start the hearings; it was on the turbine laboratory up at Trenton. And I had only been in the bureau for about two weeks when I found myself on the Hill defending that and defending Point Mugu. Vinson looked down at me after I'd read my spiel, and we wanted $10 million. He looked over at me and said, "Can you build that place for $10 million?"

---
*Representative Carl Vinson (Democrat--Georgia), chairman of the House Armed Services Committee. Vinson was a long-time friend of the Navy.

I said, "No sir."

He said, "All right, you just want to get your nose in the tent, don't you?"

I said, "Yes Sir."

He said, "All right," and he approved it.

Q: You mention Point Mugu. Were you already into the missile development work at that point?

Admiral Pride: Yes. We were just getting going on it. We needed badly a range. Just before I took over, we'd managed to get in very wrong with the people out there. Most of the land we wanted was a ranch, a very fine piece of property. Some naval officer had gone out and said, "Oh, yes, we're going to take this over." The ranch owner's house was a very fine residence. He said, "Well, that will be our officers' club." Well right away, congressmen from there and everybody were all over us. So, I said, I'd better go out there. I found this man to be a very reasonable fellow. I said we wouldn't take over his ranch house. We could work it out somehow. It was a Sunday, and he insisted on showing me all around. I explained that we really needed this range and this was the only one that was suitable. He came around and said, "All right, will you build me a little road?" up to some place he wanted.

I said, "Sure, we'll build you a road." It just went sailing on through from then. We had a little place going on up in New Jersey out in the Pineys there. We were trying out some of our missiles there, but they weren't working very well. They were just short range compared to what we expected to have working out at Mugu.

Q: One of the real proponents of that development was Captain D. S. Fahrney.* Did you work with him?

Admiral Pride: I knew Del Fahrney very well.

Q: What do you remember about him?

Admiral Pride: Well, we were very good friends, but I felt he got off on the wrong track. He was ardently

---

*See Rear Admiral Delmer S. Fahrney, USN (Ret.), "The Birth of Guided Missiles," U.S. Naval Institute Proceedings, December 1980, pages 54-60.

advocating drones. We wasted an awful lot of money and time on that. Del was quite indignant with me. I don't imagine he's ever forgotten that, or forgiven me, because when the war was over he wanted me to recommend him for a decoration for this drone work. Well, it hadn't accomplished a thing. If it had damaged the enemy or influenced him in any way, it would have been important, but it didn't. So I would not recommend Del for a decoration. I think he's probably never forgiven me for that. But he was a very able man. I don't know why he got so hipped on drones.

Q: Well, he had been working on that before the war and maintained it was really an internal political decision, that Admiral Towers would not approve them for mass combat use.*

Admiral Pride: I don't think that at all. I was right in the middle of that whole business, and the damn things just weren't that valuable, nor reliable.

---

*Vice Admiral John H. Towers, USN, Commander Air Force Pacific Fleet from October 1942 to February 1944.

Q: What made the difference between the ineffective drones and what later became the effective guided missile?

Admiral Pride: Well, I hadn't thought of that question, but I think mainly the question of propulsion. They started off with the propeller-driven airplanes. We didn't get any really effective missiles until we got effective propulsion. Lord knows, it was hard enough to get that.

Q: How much of that happened while you were the chief of the bureau--that transition in propulsion means?

Admiral Pride: I don't think I had much of anything to do with that. I watched it come along, but I didn't influence it in any way.

Q: Were the guidance systems roughly comparable between the two?

Admiral Pride: Well no, I don't think so. The very earliest guidance systems were radio controlled, but, of course, the radio control was pretty primitive. But later on we came to the more sophisticated radio control; then it became probably more practical. I know nothing about the modern missiles at all. We were trying to get going with inertial systems. That was what I favored very strongly, because back in those days when I had a fighter squadron out in the fleet I felt that we'd better get something done about our navigation. The notion of using inertial navigation, I was pushing way back in the early Thirties. Then, of course, when I became interested in the missiles, why, we were getting into studying inertial guidance. I guess that's very sophisticated now.

Q: Well, they still use something of the same technique on surface-to-air missiles in the beam rider, illuminating the target and having the missile ride that out.

Admiral Pride: When it was decided to put the Bureau of Aeronautics and Bureau of Ordnance together, I had been out of the bureau some time.* But I think what strongly influenced the Secretary of the Navy--in fact I know it was--when the Bureau of Aeronautics and the Bureau of Ordnance couldn't agree. I think it was on the Sparrow or

---
*On 1 December 1959, the Bureau of Ordnance and the Bureau of Aeronautics were abolished, and their functions were absorbed by the newly created Bureau of Naval Weapons.

one of those things. I said if it had any wings at all, it was an Aeronautics project. The Bureau of Ordnance said, no, it was a bullet of one kind or another, and it ought to belong to them. So, Chuck Noble, I guess, was Chief of the Bureau of Ordnance at that time.* The Secretary, in effect, called us over and gave us a little talking to. He said he wished we'd get together and one or the other of us would give up. I said I wouldn't, and Chuck Noble said he wouldn't. So they could never get those two bureaus together to agree on the cognizance of certain missiles. Well, Bill Franke was a very nice gentleman.** Since he couldn't get them to agree, he decided to put the two bureaus together. By that time I was back at San Diego as ComNavAirPac. He came out to see me. We were pretty good friends. I said, "Now, what in the hell did you do that for?"

He said, "You know why. I couldn't get those people to agree."

---

*Rear Admiral Albert G. Noble, USN, Chief of the Bureau of Ordnance from 1947 to 1950.
**William B. Franke was Secretary of the Navy from 1959 to 1961. The Bureau of Naval Weapons was created during his tenure as Secretary.

I said, "Well, what did you tell Congress?" or I said, "What did they ask you up there?"

He said, "Well, of course they asked me, is this going to save any people?" And he said he had to admit it wouldn't.

I told him, "If you ever do this, you've got a fellow buying bolts in the Bureau of Ordnance and another one buying bolts over in the Bureau of Aeronautics. If you put those two bureaus together, you're not going to have one desk buying all the bolts; you're going to have those two desks and another desk over them. That's the way this business works." And that's exactly what happened. I was glad to see them separate them again. That was contemplated way back, as I recall, in 1928, and it was concluded that they wouldn't even try it then.

Q: The problem was solved another way in Polaris, just in setting up a separate office.

Admiral Pride: Yes. Gee, he did a good job there.

Q: You mentioned that you reported directly to the Secretary of the Navy.

Admiral Pride: Yes, first there was Forrestal. Then he was succeeded, as I recall, by Sullivan.*

Q: What do you recall of your dealings with them?

Admiral Pride: Oh, very amiable. I found them to be very reasonable men. Forrestal, as I look back on it now, we had those Tuesday morning meetings of the chiefs of bureau with the Secretary. Forrestal was very much interested and concerned about the supply of oil from the Near East. He foresaw an awful lot of this stuff, and it worried him very much.

Q: What do you remember of Sullivan?

Admiral Pride: We became, I think, pretty good friends. He had a lot of personal courage. I mean the business of resigning when Louis Johnson short-circuited him on the carrier.** That's the kind of fellow Sullivan was. All of them left an awful lot up to the chiefs of bureau, which is what they should have done, of course.

---

*James V. Forrestal was Secretary of the Navy from 1944 to 1947 and John L. Sullivan from 1947 to 1949.
**Secretary Sullivan resigned in protest when Secretary of Defense Louis Johnson cancelled the construction of the aircraft carrier United States.

Pride #4 -181-

Q: Did you get involved in that squabble at all over the United States, the flush-deck carrier?

Admiral Pride: No, I don't think so. No, no, I didn't.

Q: How much were you involved in the development of jet aircraft?

Admiral Pride: Quite a bit at the time, I think. I like to think so. When I took over, we were just barely getting into it. We didn't have a good engine in this country. I went over to see the Rolls-Royce people to get the Nene engine to stick in the Grumman whatever it was. Those planes were coming along.

Q: The F9F?

Admiral Pride: Yes. So, I went over to see Lord Hives, who was running the Rolls-Royce jet engine business there.* It looked like a pretty good engine to me, and it turned out to be a good engine. So we bought them. I had a hard time selling jets to the Marines. Field Harris, I think, was the bull Marine aviator at that time.** I went

---
* E. W. Hives, managing director of Rolls-Royce Ltd.
** Major General Field Harris, USMC, Director of Marine Corps Aviation from July 1944 to February 1948.

over to talk about contracts for aircraft for them. They just loved the F8F or whatever was that last Grumman thing with the propeller on it.

Q: The Bearcat.

Admiral Pride: Yes. He said they wanted more of those. I said, "Look, Field, either you guys are going to fly jets or you're going out of business, because everybody else is going to fly jets." And, he wasn't so sure, but I guess some of his people talked him into it, because he gave up and we bought them some jets.

Of course, that's one thing I've found in trying to get new programs through ever since I was in the Navy. It's fashionable to say, "Well, you'll have trouble with the old hands." That's not so! My trouble was always with the people, oh, along about commander or lieutenant commander. They wanted to use whatever they were using that was good. They just wanted to keep on using it. I got more opposition from juniors than I ever did from seniors in trying to get new programs in.

Q: How would you explain that?

Admiral Pride: It's working good, and they're comfortable with it. I don't think very many people are very visionary anyway. I remember in the lower left-hand drawer of my desk there was one long discourse by one of the division heads in the bureau--you were asking about jets--explaining that you could never use jets off a carrier. It was about half an inch thick. I had put that in the lower left-hand drawer. I said, "We'll buy some jets." He was a captain, and he was supposed to be a pretty good one too, but he sure was cockeyed on that one. Well, he wasn't the only one. There were a lot of people out in the fleet that were very dubious about getting the damned things back up to revs again after you came in for a landing and you had to take a waveoff. They were quite convinced that the jet would never be able to take a waveoff. Well, I said, "By God, they'll have to or be made to, or we might as well go out of business now."

Q: Would you classify yourself as a visionary?

Admiral Pride: Oh, somewhat. Not very radical. No, I liked new ideas. After all, when I worked up the arresting gear, first for the Langley and later for the hydraulic gear for the later ships, people were predicting, "Well, you won't ever land a fighting aircraft on a ship." And, I knew damn well you'd have to.

Q: Jets were small potatoes, because you remembered a time when people said you couldn't operate planes from ships.

Admiral Pride: Yes.

Q: Did the onset of the Korean War bring new requirements for BuAer?

Admiral Pride: Yes. Well, right away just quantity-wise. But fortunately we had some airplanes left over from World War II that were available. But, of course, one of the main difficulties in those days was the refusal, on the part of the administration, to recognize the cost of the war and insist that you run a war with the normal appropriations. That held us back.

Q: How did you overcome that?

Admiral Pride: Never did overcome it, really. I would say we did the best we could. Well, one of the costs of it was that our maintenance was impaired. If you had a ceiling on the number of dollars and you put it into a new airplane, you didn't have it to fix up an old one. And, of course, that showed up, I think, particularly after the war, after Korea had quieted down, when not for probably two or three years maybe after that, but then it showed up. We had that period in there in which the maintenance of everything in the Navy was very low.

Q: Were you involved in the reactivation of the Essex-class carriers for the war? Did that come under BuAer at all?

Admiral Pride: No, I really didn't have anything to do with that.

Q: On these new aircraft projects, where would the impetus come from --the Navy, the manufacturers, or some combination?

Admiral Pride: Which impetus?

Q: Well, let's say for jets, or for a new aircraft of any type.

Admiral Pride: Well, I think that the Navy itself, but, of course, the boys from the manufacturers were always coming in and wanting to sell something, too. There was one not very good aspect to that which I suspect still may be going on. That was especially after the law when the bureau chief became the technical assistant to the Chief of Naval Operations. We had a bad time in there for a while. As a matter of fact, then the salesmen that used to come to the bureau began to go over to the Chief of Naval Operations boys and tried to sell them, not so much on complete airplanes as on the black boxes to go into the airplanes. The outstanding example of the way that worked was that miserable Vought aircraft with wings that changed their incidence. Well, anyway this airplane started out at 28,000 pounds, and it was a good airplane. The salesmen began to go over to operations, and operations would demand we put another piece of equipment in this airplane. Well, I began to protest. When it got up to 36,000 pounds from 28,000, I said, "This airplane will probably not take off of a deck anymore." I think they got it up to about 43,000, and it wouldn't. So I cancelled the contract. I wish I could remember the name of that airplane, but I can't.

Q: Was it a fighter?

Admiral Pride: Yes. After I got out in the Seventh Fleet one of the salesman, I've forgotten what he was for, oh, I guess it was from Vought, he came out. They used to come out every now and then to the fleet. He said, "Well, we got the contract reinstated." And it was a miserable airplane. It was overweight. It would be very hard to resist one of those salesmen. He comes in, he's got a new black box, and if you'll put that in your airplane it will do something. It will see the enemy, or make the bombs hit, or something or other. Yes, it would be ever so much more effective. "This increase [the phrase they used] is negligible." But you get enough of these negligible increases, and pretty soon the damned thing won't fly.

Q: There was the F7U which was strange in that it really didn't have a tail.

Admiral Pride: Maybe that was it. The way it works now, the bureau chief, I don't think, could arbitrarily cancel a contract. You'd have to have Chief of Naval Operations approval with that and probably the Secretary. You'd probably go way the hell on up to the Secretary of Defense. When I went in, we didn't have any of that overhead to go through. We could make decisions. But by the time I left, what seemed to me would be very trivial questions had to go way up, up through the Material Division, through all these other various levels. It would probably end up in the Secretary of Defense's office, which, of course, adds an awful lot of delay in actually getting stuff out to the fleet. It's very doubtful if the final decision is any better than one that's at lower levels, made because the old boy up top probably doesn't know a darn thing about it. He's relying on somebody down the line.

Q: Did you get the concerns that we see now of congressional influence on where contracts would be awarded?

Admiral Pride: I awarded a lot of contracts, and I can't imagine a single case of any congressional influence at all. No, I never was troubled that way. The awarding of a contract in those days was so much simpler than it is now. As I say, it said right there and was approved by Congress that the chief of bureau will buy the airplanes. So, you found out from Operations about how many airplanes of what type you'd like to have, and you just went ahead had your engineers draw up specifications for what you thought would be a possible airplane to meet those requirements. Then you would put that out, any number could bid on that. You usually bought three--one airplane from the three most promising designs that were submitted. You'd try them out and put the most favorable one into production.

Q: How much dealing did you have with the top men in these companies like Reuben Fleet at Consolidated, or Roy Grumman, or McDonnell?*

Admiral Pride: How much did I have with them?

Q: Right.

---
*Roy Grumman was the founder of the Grumman Aircraft Engineering Corporation, which has built a succession of fighter planes for the Navy.

Admiral Pride: A great deal. Roy and I, in World War I, went to ground school up at MIT. We had these double-decker bunks. Roy Grumman was in one deck and I was in the other. We became very good friends in ground school. And then he decided to become like a naval constructor. I think he took that course up at Cornell. I decided to stay in the line. Then after the war, when the battleships would be in for overhaul in the navy yard, we were sent out to Mitchel Field. Roy Grumman was working with a man named Loening at that time.* Loening submitted an airplane for the Navy, and we were to try it out. Roy came out then, so we resumed acquaintanceship. Then, I guess it was after I took my PG and then went to sea again. When I came ashore, I had the test section down at Hampton Roads. Roy decided to set up his own plant. It was largely financed by Loening I think. He brought his first efforts down there to Norfolk to try out. He came himself, so we saw quite a bit of each other again. Then, later on, when I had the test section at Anacostia, Roy was still working in the plant then, and I would go up frequently to see him. We were getting into the current airplanes at that time. So I knew him very well.

---

*Grover Cleveland Loening, founder of the Loening Aeronautical Engineering Corporation.

Rube Fleet was a character.* I think I became acquainted with Rube when we bought some trainers from him. I always got a bang out of him. He was an Army Air Corps officer and worked on contracts for them. He boasted, I think, that he could write a contract that would be airtight. All these contracts they always managed--well, the service itself will ask for changes. Anyway, at the end of a contract it wouldn't look much like it did at the start. He'd write contracts that these contractors never could put holes in. So then he left the Army Air Corps and went up to Buffalo. He got his training contracts up there, I think, and proceeded to shoot them full of holes.

Q: He was a very flamboyant individual, wasn't he?

Admiral Pride: Oh, yes. He was a smartie, that one. But he was a very likable person. He'd come in and have you laughing before you knew it. I saw quite a bit of him years later when I was ComAirPac out there at Coronado.**

---

*Major Reuben Fleet, a U.S. Army aviator during World War I, who founded Consolidated Aircraft Corporation in 1923.
 **Admiral Pride was Commander Air Force Pacific Fleet from 1956 to 1959.

He lived up there on Point Loma. Well, I always liked Rube very much. But I felt he was a very shrewd character. If you were talking business with him, you'd better watch yourself.

Q: The Navy was still buying seaplanes at that point. You must have had some dealings with him on that.

Admiral Pride: Yes. I think this happened when I was on the fighter class desk, which was after I got smashed up over in the test division. I think that the story goes that Mose Kraus had to do with it, then Commander Kraus.* He was having the most to do with the decision on what they'd buy. And they had a bid--I could be awfully wrong about this--the old memory is sort of weak. But I think this is about the way it was. We had bids from Rube and from Martin. Rube's bid was a little bit higher. He came in to find out how things were going, and somebody said, "Well, you're a little high." Maybe it was not an accommodation; maybe it was just that the bids were a little high. He said, "Well, all right, I'll cut it."

---
*Commander Sydney M. Kraus, USN.

Just like that, he cut the bid, and it was a lot of money, too. And he got the contract.

Q: Maybe he was doing as you were doing in Congress, just trying to get his nose in the tent.

Admiral Pride: Yes.

Q: What about McDonnell?* You probably dealt with him on the new jets.

Admiral Pride: Yes. He used to come in quite often. I think maybe his view has prevailed. His big point was that we were supplying the power plants and the communication equipment. Outside of the airframe itself, there wasn't much that wasn't government furnished. He kept trying to convince me that that was wrong. He said, "What you want is performance." All the time I was in the bureau, he worked on me to get us to buy the complete airplane. He would supply all of what we called government-furnished equipment. Well, I couldn't see it at

---
*James S. McDonnell, founder of McDonnell Aircraft Corporation.

that time. I guess I do now, but I'm not so sure that I do. Just in the matter of communication equipment, for instance, I figured if we had McDonnell supplying some stuff at his option, Grumman supplying something at his option, we'd have a conglomerate mess in there of equipment that, first off, we wouldn't be equipped to maintain, nor trained to maintain. Whereas if we supplied it, we could control the material and see that it came with our requirements for maintenance and so forth. But we'd have more control of the equipment. Well, I went against some of my own philosophy in the matter of the later reciprocating engines, though, because when I went into the bureau I'd had previous experience around there, and I knew the situation. We were demanding that we supply, oh, for instance, the fuel pumps and all kinds of little things that bolt onto an engine. We were prescribing, for instance, the specifications for the steel that goes into the crankshaft. I said, "No, we're getting into too much detail here. To be foolishly extreme, I don't care if an engine is built out of cream cheese if it performs, turns out the horsepower for the number of hours and with the economy that we have to have. I don't care what it's made out of." Which was rather contrary to my philosophy about the airplanes. But it had gone to an extreme in the matter of the old reciprocating engines, and we washed that stuff out. If Wright could turn out a better overall engine than Pratt and Whitney, which they never could, why, we'd buy it.

Q: What about your dealings with Douglas Aircraft?

Admiral Pride: I knew the old Douglas pretty well.* I became slightly acquainted with his son, who didn't pull as much water in the company as the old man had. But he was a good fellow to do business with. Yes, I always liked to do business with the Douglas company.

Q: They had the Skyraider coming along about that time, didn't they?

Admiral Pride: I think so.

Q: Ed Heinemann was their designer and turned out a series of very effective attack aircraft.**

---
*Donald Douglas, founder of Douglas Aircraft Corporation.
**Edward H. Heinemann.

Admiral Pride: Well, of course, he was a wonderful man. We had some people in the Navy whom I respect quite highly who wanted to build a jockey fighter. They felt that we had put too much into our fighters, and they wanted to strip them down. And Ed Heinemann was always wanting to make the airplane as simple as he possibly could. That was his great virtue, I thought. He was held in very high respect.

Q: The F4D was a lightweight fighter then, wasn't it?

Admiral Pride: Yes, yes. He was, again, just a very nice person to talk with and do business with.

Q: How about North American? How did things develop on the F-86 and the FJs that were used in Korea?

Admiral Pride: Well, North American turned out good equipment, but I used to have a little trouble with them. I think they are the ones I had a hard time sort of keeping the price down. I don't remember very much about them.

Pride #4 -197-

Q: Didn't the F-86 start out as an Air Force plane that the Navy then took for carrier use?

Admiral Pride: F-86? I think that's one I flew down at Patuxent. Gee, I can't remember. We ran the tests on it. If that became a carrier plane, there was considerable modification on it, as I recall. I can't recall very much about it.

Q: The angled deck, was that a development during your time?

Admiral Pride: Yes, it was. There was a project before the war, about the mid-Thirties, I guess it was, to build what they called flight deck cruisers. They wanted to keep the forward turrets. The program called for six of these ships, which never were built. But they had an angled deck so the planes wouldn't fall down and foul the turrets. Then the British came along with an angled deck, and we copied it, I said, "Gee, this reminds me of the old flight deck cruisers." But I don't think we could claim much originality for that, like so many of our things we got from the British. Some of them were disastrous, like the first carrier deck where you had the fore-and-aft wires, which we had copied from the British and they were catastrophic.

Q: What about lighter-than-air? That was pretty well phasing out by then, wasn't it?

Admiral Pride: Yes. I guess that I was the executioner. Rosendahl didn't think much of me.* But, damn it, I did keep one project going there. As I recall, it was a Goodyear ship with Chrysler engines in it. I think the engine was actually in the car and drove the propellers out through shafts. We carried that one for a while, and then I think I cancelled it. It just wasn't getting anywhere and was going to cost a lot of money. Rosendahl came down to see me and I'm afraid he wasn't very happy.

Q: Well, that had been his pet project for years.

Admiral Pride: Oh, sure, sure.

---
*Vice Admiral Charles E. Rosendahl, USN(Ret.), who had a long involvement with lighter-than-air craft in the Navy.

Q: Was it just a matter of there not being enough dollars to support all this and what else you had to do?

Admiral Pride: No, to use that horrible term that McNamara used, I didn't think that they were cost-effective.*

Q: You thought their functions could be performed better by other types of planes?

Admiral Pride: Yes.

Q: What about helicopter development? Any memories on that?

Admiral Pride: Yes. Well, to go back much further on that I'd become acquainted with Sikorsky years before that.** When I was stationed at Mitchel Field, he was building airplanes over on the adjacent field there. So I kept pretty well abreast of what he was up to. Also, this fellow who was out at College Park, Berliner.*** We were

---
*Robert S. McNamara, Secretary of Defense from 1961 to 1968.
**Igor I. Sikorsky.
***Henry Berliner.

acquainted, and I knew what was going on there. So, when I came into the bureau, I was pretty well acquainted with the rotary-wing business. In fact, when I had the test section at Hampton Roads we got the autogiros. I ran the trials on that and took one up and landed it on the Langley. So, I was pretty well versed in the rotary-wing, and I also knew the troubles they were having on it. They really didn't know what was going on in the blades as they went whirling around. But I felt that they certainly would be especially useful when we tried to transfer stuff from one ship to another in small amounts. It was always a nuisance to try to bring one ship alongside another. I felt it would be very nice to have them for that and probably for other things. So when I went into the bureau, I was all for getting some of these things. But one of the drawbacks was that the ones that we had in prospect then were all unstable. Oh, another thing, we wanted to use them for trying to find submarines at night and if you let the stick go on one of these things, you went into a catastrophe right away. They were not stable. One day, the Secretary called up on the squawk box and he said, "There is a young fellow up in Connecticut who has a helicopter that he thinks you might be interested in. Would you take a look at it?"

I said, "Sure, I'll look at a helicopter any time."

Well, it turned out to be Charley Kaman.* He came in to see me, and they described his helicopter to me.

And I said, "Is it stable?"

They said, "It is." It had the counter-rotating propellers. So I asked him to bring it down, and he brought it down. There was no fabric on the sides. It was just a framework affair. We went up and flew the thing around. I could take my hands off the stick, and the damn thing was perfectly stable. He indicated that he just about didn't have any money left. So I said, "How much of a contract would you need to keep you in business?"

He said, "Oh, if I could get $35,000."

I said, "I think we can fix that. "I went back to the Bureau to whatever division did such things, and said, "Give Kaman a contract for $35,000 to develop the blade itself." They needed some work on that, and that was how he got started. Of course, now he's doing not very much

---

*Charles H. Kaman, president of Kaman Corporation.

helicopter business, but a lot of other things, making guitars and such like.

Q: Well, he reactivated his helicopter line.

Admiral Pride: Has he?

Q: For antisubmarine warfare, the SH-2.

Admiral Pride: Well, he went away from the counter-rotating propellers. I was amused, one day we were at lunch down there with some organization. There was quite a room full of people. But Igor Sikorsky was on one side of me, and the fellow with the flying bananas, Frank Piasecki, was on the other side. Pretty soon they were just talking about their respective types and Sikorsky says," Oh, but you have to have two propellers, two rotors."

And the other man says, "But, Igor, you've got two rotors"--meaning the big one and the little one on the tail. Piasecki was an excellent engineer, but he didn't run his finances too well. He was more interested in the engineering.

One day, one of the Rockefellers--was it Laurance?--and about a half a dozen of these young men had got together, and they had set up a little company. They were all wealthy people. They were looking around for outfits that were having a hard time but had a good product. He came in one day and said, "I hear you're having some trouble with this outfit, they're up in New Jersey, but you want their helicopters."

I said, "You're right."

He said, "Well, would you like us to take a hand in running the place and straighten them out?"

I said, "I sure as heck would."

So he did and they, as far as I know, are still making them.

Q: Did you have much involvement with the Coast Guard when you were in that job?

Admiral Pride: Oh, just sort of socially is all.

Q: If they got an aircraft that was the same as one the Navy was buying, would they just follow your lead on that?
Admiral Pride: Yes. Well, yes. I've forgotten. What's

the name of that flying boat they had? I remember that one of their contracts that went right along with one of ours and probably reduced the cost for all of us. But I think that they could always probably, in those days, get a cheaper airplane because it didn't have to do as many things as ours did.

Q: There was one flying boat. I think HU-16 or something like that.

Admiral Pride: Yes. Of course, in World War I, I served at a station in France that had a Coast Guard captain and so had Chatham, Massachusetts, when I came back there.

Q: How much dealing did you have with the Deputy Chief of Naval Operations for Air, OP-05?

Admiral Pride: Not very much other than for requirements. In those days, as I say, I made all the congressional appearances. After all, he was concerned with operations. I was not. I was concerned with supplying the stuff so he could operate and try to keep it going.

Q: How much dealing did you have with the training establishment in getting things set up for the new aircraft that were coming on line?

Admiral Pride: There again, I had almost no direct dealings with them. They apparently told Operations they needed so many training planes of such a type. Operations would pass the word to me, and then we'd try to draw up a specification to meet their requirements, and try to get the money to buy them.

Q: Any more on your BuAer time? I think I've about exhausted my questions on that phase.

Admiral Pride: Yes.

Q: You got another carrier division after that. Wasn't that sort of unusual to get a second shot?

Admiral Pride: I guess they didn't know what to do with me. I loved the carrier division. I liked operating the carriers, the groups at sea, just operating them.

Q: This was CarDiv Two. Was it again a case of operating back and forth between the Sixth Fleet and the East Coast?

Admiral Pride: Yes, after World War II I didn't get back to the West Coast, I think, until I went to the Seventh Fleet.

Q: When you were over in the Mediterranean, for whom were you working?

Admiral Pride: Let's see, Admiral Carney was the senior one over there then.* My immediate senior was Matt Gardner.**

Q: Well, he was about a contemporary of yours, wasn't he?

Admiral Pride: Yes, he was of the Naval Academy class that was junior. I'm between two classes, and he was a member of the class junior to mine. But he'd been fleeted up, so I was reporting to him.***

---
*Admiral Robert B. Carney, USN, Commander Naval Striking Forces Southern Europe.
**Vice Admiral Matthias B. Gardner, USN, Commander Sixth Fleet.
***Admiral Gardner was in the Naval Academy class of 1919.

Q: Carney was CinCSouth during the Fifties.

Admiral Pride: Yes. I know when I would be in Naples I would call on Mick.

Q: What was your mission then--showing the flag?

Admiral Pride: Yes, I think that was probably it. Of course, we had our exercises. We also were having these joint exercises with the other nations there. I remember one exercise we had, and included what I think was the Netherlands ship, a fairly small one. I thought to myself, "Now, what am I going to do with him?" So I made him a guide. He stayed right in the middle of the formation all the time.

Q: This was connected with NATO?

Admiral Pride: Yes, that was when we were getting NATO going. That was one of our functions. For instance, we used the NATO signals, which was my first experience with them. It went pretty smoothly, though. I was very gratified. They assigned tactical command to the carrier division commanders. And the Sixth Fleet Commander stayed pretty well clear, though there were usually two carrier division commanders there. I would have, say, tactical command for a month, and the other fellow would have it for a month, like that. Yes, I think that was one of our functions, to try to get this NATO business going navy-wise.

Q: What language did you communicate in?

Admiral Pride: Well, most of the time we just used signals. And the signals, of course, were interpreted in the different books. But if I had occasion to use a language, I used English. All over the world now, everybody can communicate in English. That's been my experience. When I was later in the Seventh Fleet, there was no trouble at all.

Q: That's fortunate for us.

Admiral Pride: Yes, yes. Well, sometimes you feel a little bit guilty about this. You feel that maybe you're a little lazy.

Q: Were there any differences in the pattern of operations in the 1950s from what you'd experienced back right after World War II?

Admiral Pride: Yes, I would say there was quite a difference. The advent of the steam catapult made the ship less dependent on wind, or gave them more liberty in their launching operations. Yes, I saw launches later on which we wouldn't have been able to make without the steam catapult--again from the British.

Q: Wasn't the Sixth Fleet bigger by then also than it had been?

Admiral Pride: Let's see, was it? I'm not so sure that it was. I can't remember very well. It seemed to me it was about the same.

Q: Was "Cat" Brown operating over there when you were?*

Admiral Pride: Yes.

---

*Rear Admiral Charles R. Brown, USN, later Commander Sixth Fleet.

Q: Another colorful character. What do you remember about him?

Admiral Pride: Yes. Well, I think that I was very much amused when it came time for "Cat" and, "Artie" Doyle to turn over a job at Gibraltar.* They had their two respective flagships there. Messages went back and forth. Artie Doyle, I guess, was turning over to "Cat" and he said, "All right, 10:00 o'clock tomorrow morning is all right, but you'll have to wear shoes." You know how it is in a carrier. You don't know who's coming up the ladder or what his condition is until he shows up on the hangar deck. So the next morning there was the parade and the guard and the band and everything, all these formalities. Artie stood there. Pretty soon "Cat's" head appeared at the top of the ladder, holding his shoes up in his hands. This was supposed to be a very dignified and stuffy operation.

When we put the Langley in commission in '22, "Cat" was one of the deck officers. I think there were six of us aviators on the ship at the time. He saw that we had

---
*Rear Admiral Austin K. Doyle, USN.

a pretty good racket going, so he decided he'd become an aviator, too. He and Jack Tate.*

Q: Well, what do you recall of Jack Tate? He also was very colorful.

Admiral Pride: Oh, I should say so. We served together at various times. I was always wondering what was going to happen next. Jack had a peculiar faculty. He could tell the truth and make it sound like a lie. I've seen him make innumerable bets. He'd make one of these apparently atrocious statements, and it was so obvious that he was wrong that anybody around would say, "I'll bet you $5.00 that you're wrong." And he would collect.

Q: Apparently he did some pretty impossible things that people wouldn't believe could have happened.

Admiral Pride: Yes, yes. He was with a flag officer over in the Mediterranean before he was an aviator? He had a destroyer. Or was it the Isabel? I've forgotten which

---

*Ensign Jackson R. Tate, USN, was assigned to the destroyer Borie (DD-215), operating in the Black Sea in 1920.

one it was. I've forgotten the complications, but it seems to me--oh, I know. This old rear admiral, Jack was his aide. This fellow had adopted some Russian children, and he brought them out to the ship and turned them over to Jack to take charge.* Well, Jack put them all in the chart house and locked the door and figured there he would know where they were. When he went to release them they had managed to get out all the charts and colored pencils and had ruined the place.

I always liked one of Jack's stories. It was in the same ship. I think it was one of the old four-stack destroyers. He said that one evening, remembering you could look down the companionway there and see into the little wardroom and see the officers eating, the officers were down there, and they were having artichokes. The gangway watch looked down, a boatswain's mate, and said, "Them officers eats the god-damnedest things."

Q: Did you have any dealings with Admiral Radford during the course of your career?**

---

*Probably Rear Admiral Newton A. McCully, USN, who was on special assignment in London.
**Admiral Arthur W. Radford, USN.

Admiral Pride: Not very much. I knew him. Well, I guess I did at that. I had quite a bit to do with him. He was the Chairman of the Joint Chiefs of Staff when I had the Seventh Fleet. He came out then. But I'd known him since we were both lieutenants.

Q: He has been described as a very highly professional individual.

Admiral Pride: Oh, yes. Yes indeed.

Q: Well, you were along together on that Howland and Baker operation in 1943, I think.

Admiral Pride: I was in that with the Belleau Wood. Yes. We were disappointed and didn't see some Japs. Probably just as well.

Q: When you were in the Sixth Fleet, was there any sense that you had been deprived of some ships because they were needed in Korea instead?

Admiral Pride: I never felt that particularly.

Q: I'm surprised that the Midway-class ships continued to deploy to the Sixth Fleet rather than going to Korea. What considerations were involved?

Admiral Pride: I have no idea. I haven't any idea why that was. Of course, I think it was a very serious thought in those days that maybe the Russians would come south, and if they did, we'd have to put up a pretty good fight. We had some plans made up for that event. I think that in some minds that was probably an even more serious concern than what was going on in Korea.

Q: Well, that could well be the explanation then. How much did tactical nuclear weapons play a part in your planning for that area?

Admiral Pride: A great deal. What were those airplanes called "Pride's Folly," that we had that were supposed to carry things?

Q: Well, it was the AJ.*

---
*The AJ was a Navy attack plane, designed specifically to carry atomic bombs.

Admiral Pride: Yes. Well, I realized the deficiency there, but I had put that contract through in the bureau, because at that time the only weapon we had was that big round bomb, and we didn't have an airplane that would carry the thing. So, I said Well, we'd better get something that will lug this thing and get it as quick as we can." So that's why I went for that contract. Yes, we had them over there.

Q: What was the doctrine as far as the use of the weapons? Would that come down from the President?

Admiral Pride: Yes, that had to come from the President.
An interesting thing about that when I was out in the Seventh Fleet. We ran one exercise there, a fleet exercise, most of it around the east coast of Taiwan. Just east of Taiwan. The Chinese were very successful in blanking out our communications. In fact, the Nationalists blanked their own out. They had no radio discipline, and they turned everything on full speed. I complained about that to the "Gimo" and rectified some of that.* Anyway, in this one exercise, which was, I think, the first one that involved using the weapons against the
----
   *"Gimo" was a nickname for Generalissimo Chiang Kai-Shek.

mainland, our communications were completely blanked out. To get a message out, I had to put it in an airplane and send it up to Okinawa and transmit it from there. I thought, "This is going to be one hell of a fix if I can't tell them back there what's going on, and they can't get word back to me if I could." Well, it got better later, but still we had awfully heavy interference. I thought it was a very serious thing.

Q: Did you interpret it as deliberate on the part of the Red Chinese?

Admiral Pride: Oh, yes, undoubtedly. As soon as the exercise was over, why, everything cleared right up again.

Q: That's a good indication.

Admiral Pride: Of course, we used them somewhat. We didn't have at that time any good Chinese interpreters in the Navy. I borrowed them from the Army. They trained them at Fort Ord. We read their radio quite well. But then the rascals got to sending an awful lot of stuff by landline, and, of course, we couldn't get that. But when we had taken those troops and people off the islands--

when I had our carriers and the whole damned fleet out there, the Red Chinese were watching this thing very closely and chattering among themselves. I'd learn when the planes had left our carriers quicker via the Red Chinese than I would by our own communications. The carriers were quite far out, a hundred miles. But they knew when these things were going on. But I could fox them sometimes in those days. I suppose you couldn't do it now with the satellite and everything. But Taiwan's mountains would go up to about 10,000 feet, and I could operate down in the lee of Taiwan, to the east, and it obviously hampered their surveillance like everything.

Q: When you had those nuclear weapons in the Sixth Fleet, was there any concern for security on board ship?

Admiral Pride: Oh, I couldn't go look at them. You bet your life there was. Nobody but the people involved could have the slightest access to them.

Q: After that tour, you went to Naval Air Test Center, which by then had moved to Patuxent River.

Admiral Pride: That's right.

Q: I would think the logical operation would be to have that command before you had BuAer.

Admiral Pride: Well, it would be.

Q: Why the flip-flop?

Admiral Pride: They didn't know what to do with me. I was sort of a spare pump handle, and that place was available. They asked if I'd take it, and I said, "Sure."

Q: Well, it certainly was something that you were well prepared for.

Admiral Pride: Yes. Yes, I felt like I could do the job all right.

Q: What experiences come to your mind from that period?

Admiral Pride: Well, I don't know. I can't think of anything of any moment at all. We had a facility there for loading the weapons which I was very much concerned about. I wasn't so sure it would be adequate. But I didn't get anything straightened out. I can't think of anything of any particular moment. It was a very pleasant duty.

Q: What planes were being tested then? Do you recall?

Admiral Pride: Let's see, what did we do?

Q: That may have been the time that the F8U was.

Admiral Pride: I think it was. I can't remember just what was going on. I enjoyed very much flying the, what was that? The F-86, was it? We had two or three of them down there and stripped everything out of them. They surely were sweet airplanes.

When I went into the bureau, I said,"I don't think any flag officers have flown a jet. So I called up Patuxent and said, "Have you got something down there?" Well, the only thing they had at that time was that first thing we got. What was it? A Consolidated with two engines in it.* I said, "Well, I'm coming down and fly the thing." So I went down, and, of course, I didn't know

----
*Admiral Pride's log shows that on 25 April 1947, he flew a YP-59, a Consolidated plane which did not go into production.

anything about jets. But, all at once, I said, "This is swell," and I got up in the air. I was used to the old propeller driven things and you were always pushing on one foot or the other to counteract the torque. Here was something that had no torque. It was so pleasant to fly. I was out over the bay there, and all at once one engine stopped, but I wasn't sure which engine it was. I wasn't too familiar with the cockpit. Anyway, I called up the station and said "I've lost one engine, so I think I'd better come on in." They agreed with me. I could have just as well have put the thing into the bay, I suppose. I got it back. But that was my first jet experience.

Q: I think the general reaction is that it's easier to fly a jet than a reciprocating one.

Admiral Pride: Absolutely. Yes.

Q: So you were the first Navy flag officer to fly a jet?

Admiral Pride: Yes, yes.

Q: I know you have many other firsts.

Admiral Pride: Dan Gallery said, "Did you fly a jet?"

I said, "Yes."

He flew the next one, I think.

Q: Well, he was very much involved in that big unification squabble there after the war. Did that touch you at all?

Admiral Pride: No, it really didn't. I watched it going on, but I had nothing to do with it at all.

Q: Well, then it came time you got command of the Seventh Fleet. Did that surprise you after you had been treated as a spare pump handle?

Admiral Pride: Yes. Mick Carney called and said, "How would you like to go out and command the Seventh Fleet?"

I said, "You must be crazy." I was delighted to get that.

Q: Did he say why he had chosen you?

Admiral Pride: No, and doesn't say to this day. I see him occasionally.

Pride #4 -222-

Q: It was traditionally at that point an aviator's command and you obviously were the right seniority.

Admiral Pride: Oh, yes, yes.

Q: Wasn't "Jocko" Clark a hard act to follow?*

Admiral Pride: Oh, I didn't find him hard to follow. I didn't approve of some of the things he did. For instance, he had the flag in the battleship. He had something like 140 officers on his staff. I knew that was ridiculous. I didn't ask for the flag to be taken off the battleship, but it was decided to put it in a cruiser. That gave me an immediate excuse to cut the staff right in half. I cut it down to 70 officers. Of course, we got the work done that much more rapidly.

Q: You didn't have as much internal circulation.

Admiral Pride: No, no. Yes, "Jocko" had done a fine job out there, especially in support of the Korean operations. I was told later that they were at some conference, and

---
*Vice Admiral Joseph J. Clark, USN, Commander Seventh Fleet from May 1952 until December 1953.

some of the Army officers were saying, "We've got to do this and we've got to do that."

And, "Jocko" said, "I think we've got to kill a lot of Chinamen, and I'm going back to the ship." And he promptly started his Cherokee raids, or whatever they were.

Q: Well, what were the contrasts in living conditions? I think you went from the Wisconsin to the Rochester, was it?

Admiral Pride: Yes. Oh, I was perfectly comfortable. I still had room enough to have about ten people in my mess. It was so much more convenient with a smaller staff.

Q: What are the reasons for the large staff? Had it been the Korean War? Was it inevitable that it would have gotten smaller?

Admiral Pride: No, it wasn't inevitable. "Jocko" could have reduced it, because the fighting was pretty well over. I don't think it bothered "Jocko" at all. He wasn't concerned with that.

Q: Well, after the war ended was the Taiwan patrol your main concern? The relations between that and the mainland?

Admiral Pride: Yes, I think so. There were little incidents occurring all over the place all the time. The Nationalists would make some sort of a little raid on some establishment along the coast. The Tachens had to be evacuated, and things like that. Then maybe the Reds would step up their bombarding of Quemoy. That would get people sort of worked up. There again, it was the business of communications. It was quite interesting. One of these little incidents would pop up, and I'd report it and maybe have to take some action. Then about two days later, a message would come through, "Why did you do this?" Felix Stump was back in Pearl at that time, and he would always jump into it and say, "I have complete confidence in Commander Seventh Fleet and approve of what he did."* So that would end the whole thing. But the point I'm trying to make is that the fellow that's out there does not get an instant reply. Things can happen just in 24 hours. Things can develop, but you can't get

---
*Admiral Felix B. Stump, USN, Commander in Chief Pacific Fleet.

an answer back from here in 24 hours. It usually has to go up through the Navy Department, the State Department, and maybe the Secretary of Defense gets into the act, and maybe it gets to the White House. It has to come all the way back down again. So the commander in the field, if he's any distance from Washington, can very well get into a situation where he's got to take action that may or may not be approved.

Q: Do you recall any examples of that sort of thing that happened--where you had to move on without waiting for directions?

Admiral Pride: Oh, yes. Well, for instance, during the Tachens operation. One of our planes foolishly got in where he shouldn't have been and got shot down. Right away, the newspaper people were all around there asking, "What are you going to do about it?" Well, I couldn't wait for a report that never came back. I had to make my decision. I said, "Well, the guy misnavigated, and he got shot down. I'm not going to do anything about it." The whole thing blew over. Now, if I'd decided to make something out of it and take a shot at some of those people where it was clearly our own fault, as I told the people right around there, "If one of their planes came over our operation we'd shoot him down." Then there was another occasion; I think the Chinese Nationalists sent one of their vessels in and attacked one of the more southern islands. For a moment there, it looked like a critical situation. Should we support them if things did blow up after all? They had no justification for doing it whatsoever. We had that treaty with them, the mutual treaty. Or should we just stay clear of it? I decided to just stay clear of the whole situation. It just blew over, and that was that. It's very hard, I think, in those situations. A lot depends on just keeping your cool and don't make it any worse.

Q: How much tactical control, if any, does the fleet commander have?

Admiral Pride: It would vary with individuals, I imagine. I enjoyed exercising quite a bit of it. I normally wouldn't say, "Launch your aircraft at such and such a time," or anything like that. I prescribed the fleet formation and the courses and left it up to the individual group commanders to decide the details of their aircraft operation. But you take charge usually in refueling, resupply operations; prescribed formations, times, speeds, courses, and all that sort of thing.

Q: Well, the fleet is so large, of course, you couldn't gather it all at once. How much touch did you keep with all the outlying elements?

Admiral Pride: It depends if they've got radio silence or not. If you haven't got radio silence, they usually give you the word of something that changes. You don't converse with them very much. They are responsible people. If they have something come up unusual, a breakdown or something like that, they'll let you know.

Q: How big a part did your relationship with the Taiwanese Government play in your overall job as Commander Seventh Fleet?

Admiral Pride: I think the dominant consideration was our support of the Chinese, not the native Taiwanese. It bothers me in the paper, they keep mixing up the

Nationalist Chinese and the Taiwanese Chinese. There's, of course, a great deal of difference. The Taiwanese left China something over 300 years ago. In my day, of course, we were always speculating on what was going to become of the Nationalist Chinese. It was an article of faith with Chiang Kai-shek that they would go back to the mainland. I don't think any of us really believed that. However, we were very much concerned in those days with the possibility of an attack by the Red Chinese on Taiwan. We drew up plans for what we'd do in that event. We were also concerned, of course, with what should be done if the Chinese decided to take over Hong Kong. In that case, we realized that they probably would be successful right away, and our main problem would be to get the Americans out of there and such of the other nationals as wished to come. So we had our plans drawn up for that. I felt personally that the Russians might decide to attack the Japanese. The Russians were hanging onto the northern islands there which had been Japanese. I went up and looked over that situation where they would probably land. There are some beautiful beaches up there if you want to make an amphibious landing. So I think that these are some of the considerations that in those days we had on our minds in trying to make plans for what we ought to do

Pride #4 -229-

in case something happened. Of course, the only thing that did happen, probably, was, and it seems relatively minor now, was when the Red Chinese decided to take over the northern islands.

Q: What were your relations with the Japanese during that period?

Admiral Pride: Very cordial. Very cordial. In fact, I still correspond with a fellow that became their Chief of Naval Operations. Of course, they didn't have very much there. They had their self-defense force or whatever they called it. We used Sasebo, and we did an awful lot of work at Yokosuka.

Q: What about the Philippines? How much relationship with them?

Admiral Pride: Almost none. Very little. I'd go down to Subic Bay occasionally. I never saw any government officials except on social occasions.

Q: How much of your activity was governed by the State Department inputs? Or would those come via the Defense Department rather than directly?

Admiral Pride: Of course, I probably couldn't tell. They always had some of their representatives around and, oh, on a lot of occasions, for instance--I didn't have any of those, although I was very friendly with some of the Japanese, but mostly their military people. And, one who turned out to be very close friends was Hollington Tong, who was the Chinese ambassador to Japan at that time. We saw quite a bit of each other. Well, on one occasion, to get away from the Japanese a moment and back to the Chinese, we were getting some intelligence, or our State Department was, from the Nationalist Chinese. They were getting it from Red China, intercepting it and then interpreting it. Our State Department said, "We don't want their interpretation. What we want is the raw material and we'll interpret it." So Dulles asked me to see Chiang Kai-shek, not number one Dulles, but his brother.

Q: Allen Dulles.*

Admiral Pride: Yes. So, I would see Chiang Kai-shek about it. I used to go up and see him about once a week

---

*Allen Dulles was Director of the Central Intelligence Agency.

Pride #4 -231-

if I was around Taiwan anyway. I explained it to him. He said, "All right, we'll give them the raw material." So they did. But that's about the only direct business I ever did for the State Department. Of course, I was very friendly with the ambassador.

Q: You went from there to NavAirPac, again into an aviation billet. Did you enjoy that transition?

Admiral Pride: Oh, sure. That's a very pleasant billet. I was there over three years, I think, enjoying every minute of it.

Q: What were your primary duties there?

Admiral Pride: Mostly material and training. We had the reserve air group there. There was the getting the groups ready to go out and providing material.

Q: You probably worked with First Fleet Commander a fair amount, didn't you?

Admiral Pride: Oh, yes. I don't think either of us had very arduous duties.

Q: Are there any particular incidents from that period that you recall?

Admiral Pride: No, I don't think of anything in particular. As I say, it's so long ago now it's all pretty hazy. I can't think of any time when I was terribly anxious about something or waiting for something to happen.

Q: Was it sort of anticlimactic after having a fleet command?

Admiral Pride: Oh, yes. Sure. In fact I think the word command has been terribly abused throughout the Navy Department. Possibly in the Army and Air Force, too. Because in actual exercising command, ComNavAirPac really doesn't command much of anything. He is an administrator, but he doesn't issue any commands. The deployment schedule says when your reserve groups go somewhere or something like that. You make sure that they are ready to go. I think all this is foolishness in calling the various materiel operations "commands." I can't see it. I would much prefer to have kept the word "command" and reserved it for military commands.

Q: Well, you didn't have that title when you were in the Bureau of Aeronautics because then it was still called chief.

Admiral Pride: Sure.

Q: More appropriate.

Admiral Pride: Much more appropriate.

Q: There was one individual that you talked about only in passing in the earlier interviews that I would enjoy hearing more about, and that's Marc Mitscher.*

Admiral Pride: Oh, of course, I enjoyed my acquaintance with him very much. He was a very reserved type, except occasionally when it was just the two of us in the mess there most of the time. And, occasionally he would get into a sort of talking jag. But most of the time he was

---

*In 1937 and 1938, Commander Marc A. Mitscher, USN, was commanding officer of the seaplane tender Wright (AV-1) and Pride was the ship's air officer.

very reserved. He demanded a very high level of performance, too. If you were doing your work, and doing it satisfactorily, he left you strictly alone. He never asked why did you do this or anything like that. He saved my bacon for me, too. Because of this game leg, I had a much more pronounced limp than I do now. I have some now, but it was very pronounced. After all, when I went to the Wright, Pete Mitscher was the captain of the Wright. I went to her as air officer. Henry Mullinnix was the executive officer.* Well, when I went to go to the Wright I removed the iron brace from my leg. They have a pretty good union down there. It bent a little bit. I was a lieutenant commander, and I had been selected for commander. But the months went by and I didn't get my commission. Other selectees who were junior to me had theirs. So, I wrote a letter to the Bureau of Navigation. I said, "Why haven't I got my commission?"

They wrote back and said, "You don't have your commission, and you're not going to get it, because you have an unsatisfactory fitness report."

---

*Commander Henry M. Mullinnix, USN, who later became a rear admiral and was lost when his flagship, the USS Liscome Bay, was torpedoed during the Tarawa operation in December 1943.

I wrote back and said, "What is the unsatisfactory fitness report?" The fitness report had been made out by the executive officer, and Pete apparently signed it without realizing what he was doing. It had very good marks all the way down, but in the remarks it said, "He has a limp which does not affect his duty materially." They said that constituted an unsatisfactory report. So I took it up to Mitscher, and I said, "Well, I guess I'm not going to be a commander. I guess I ought to get out of this outfit."

He just nodded his head and said, "Well, let me take it."

So pretty soon I got my commission. I don't know how he did it, because you're not supposed to be able to change a fitness report. But he did it somehow.

Q: You had a lot of good luck all along the line.

Admiral Pride: Yes, yes, that's what it was.

Q: Well, I think that's a good note to end it on.

Index to
Reminiscences of
Admiral Alfred M. Pride
U.S. Navy (Retired)

Accidents--Aviation
    Problems with early aircraft carrier arresting gear in the 1920s, pp. 30-32; Pride injured seriously when he crashed an XO3U-6 in the Potomac River in 1934, 97-99, 105, 107, 167-168; barrier crash which killed a gun crew on board the light carrier Belleau Wood (CVL-24) in World War II, p. 134; crash of an H-boat seaplane in the Connecticut River in 1919, pp. 169-171

Aeronautical Board
    Pride's service in the 1930s with this U.S. Government agency which established standard aviation specifications and licensed equipment for foreign sales, pp. 92-96

Aeronautics, Bureau of
    Supervision of naval aviation development work in the late 1920s, pp. 76-77, 81-82; drew up specifications for Navy planes and worked with aircraft manufacturers in the 1930s, pp. 103-104, 108-112, 192-193; Pride's tenure as chief of the bureau from 1947 to 1951, pp. 161-162, 171-189, 193-205; merger with the Bureau of Ordnance in 1959, pp. 177-179; law changed in the late 1940s so the bureau reported to OpNav rather than SecNav, p. 186

Air Corps, U.S. Army
    Trained Navy pilots to fly land planes soon after World War I, pp. 17-18, 163; represented on national Aeronautical Board in the 1930s, pp. 94-95; contact with the Navy's Bureau of Aeronautics in the 1930s, pp. 110-111; Reuben Fleet as contracting officer for shortly after World War I, p. 191

    See also: Air Forces, U.S. Army

Aircraft
    Modification of land planes in the 1920s for use on board aircraft carriers, pp. 42-43; experiments with landing treads and skis on planes around 1930, pp. 81-82; new models tested by the Navy in the 1930s after development by manufacturers, pp. 89-91, 97-107; role of the Aeronautical Board in the 1930s in setting specifications and licensing aviation equipment for overseas sales, pp. 93-96

    See also: Aeronautics, Bureau of; Air Corps, U.S. Army; Air Forces, U.S. Army; Autogiro; Bombers; Dive-bombers; Fighter Planes; Flying Boats; Seaplanes

Aircraft Carriers
    Development of the USS Langley (CV-1) as the Navy's first carrier in the 1920s and 1930s, pp. 27-37, 39-44, 53, 56, 61-63, 68, 88-89; fitting out and initial service of the USS Lexington (CV-2) which went into commission in 1927, pp. 51-61, 63-68, 73-74; development of carriers by foreign navies in the 1920s, pp. 67-69; decision concerning the tonnage of the Lexington and Saratoga (CV-3) to comply with treaty requirements in the 1920s, pp. 69-71; Saratoga operations in the Pacific in 1941 and at the outset of World War II, pp. 71-72, 120-124; development of deck lighting system and deck tie-down system in the late 1920s, pp. 80-81; evaluation of the role of carriers in the Navy of the 1930s, pp. 116-117; fitting out and initial service of the USS Belleau Wood (CVL-24), which went into commission in 1943, pp. 122, 125-134; operations of Carrier Divisions Six and Four in the Atlantic and Mediterranean in 1946-1947, pp. 147-148, 153-161; comparison of the characteristics of various classes of carriers, pp. 151-152; feeling by some officers in the late 1940s that jet aircraft could not operate from carriers, p. 183; adoption by the U.S. Navy in the 1950s of the angled deck developed by the British, p. 197; operations of Carrier Division Two in the Atlantic and Mediterranean in 1951-1952, pp. 205-209, 213-215

Aircraft Design
    Differences between conventional land planes and carrier planes in the 1920s and 1930s, pp. 90-91; in the 1960s, p.92; role of the Aeronautical Board in establishing standard specifications in the 1930s, pp. 93-96; specifications for Navy planes in the 1930s were drawn up by the Bureau of Aeronautics, pp. 103-104, 108-111; work of designer Edward Heinemann of Douglas Aircraft Corporation, pp. 195-196

Aircraft Engines
    Aeronautical Board divided engine development work between the Army and the Navy in the 1930s, p. 94; role of engines in overall aircraft design in the 1930s, p. 104; development of jet aircraft by the U.S. Navy in the late 1940s and early 1950s, pp. 181-183

Aircraft Manufacturers
    New planes tested by the Navy at Hampton Roads around 1930 after development by manufacturers, pp. 89-91; tested by Flight Test Section at Anacostia during Pride's command tenure in the mid-1930s, pp. 99-102, 105-107; design and construction of new planes to meet Navy specifications in the 1930s, pp. 103-104, 111-112; relationship with the Navy in the late 1940s and early 1950s, pp. 186-187, 189, 193-201

See also: Fleet, Reuben; Grumman, Roy; Kaman, Charles H.; McDonnell, James S.; Piasecki, Frank; Sikorsky, Igor

Air Force, Pacific Fleet
Role of the force commander in the late 1950s, pp. 231-232

Air Forces, U.S. Army
Bombing of Japan at the end of World War II, pp. 140-142

See also: Air Corps, U.S. Army

Air Test Center
See: Naval Air Test Center

AJ (Savage)
Bomber developed by the U.S. Navy in the late 1940s for delivery of nuclear weapons, pp. 214-215

Amphibious Operations
Plans for possible U.S. invasion of Japan at the end of World War II, pp. 138-141

Anacostia Naval Air Station
Site of Navy Flight Test Section in the mid-1930s, pp. 97-107, 111, 167-169

Arizona, USS (BB-39)

Description of the operation of the ship's spotting planes shortly after World War I, including the reaction of the Arizona's skipper, pp. 20-26, 163-166.

Army, U.S.
See: Air Corps, Air Forces

Arresting Gear
Pride assigned the task of devising flight deck arresting gear for the USS Langley (CV-1) in the early 1920s, pp. 27-36, 43-44; development of arresting gear for the Lexington (CV-2) and Saratoga (CV-3) in the 1920s, pp. 44-45, 51-53, 73-74, 83

Atlantic Fleet Ship Plane Division
Flew spotting planes from battleship turrets in the early post-World War I period, pp. 16-26, 163-166

Atomic Bombs
See: Nuclear Weapons

Autogiro
Forerunner of the helicopter tested on board the USS Langley (CV-1) in 1931, pp. 84-85

Aviation--Civilian
> Planes and pilots shortly after the beginning of the 20th century, pp. 4-5

Aviation--Naval
> Involved in patrol duty in World War I, pp. 9-10, 15; flight training in World War I, pp. 10-15; operation of spotting planes from battleships soon after World War I, pp. 16-26, 163-166; development of carrier Langley (CV-1) and arresting gear in the early 1920s, pp. 27-37, 39-45, 53, 56-57, 61-63, 68, 87; fitting out, commissioning, and early service of the USS Lexington (CV-2) in the late 1920s, pp. 51-55, 57-61, 63-67, 73-74; development of the landing signal officer (LSO) concept for carriers by Commander Kenneth Whiting in the early 1920s, pp. 61-63; development of aircraft carriers by foreign navies in the 1920s, pp. 67-69; decision concerning tonnage of the Lexington (CV-2) and Saratoga (CV-3) in 1941-1942, pp. 71-72, 120-124; development work on aircraft at the Experimental Division, Hampton Roads, in the late 1920s, pp. 74-76, 79-85, 89-91; development of dive-bombing in the 1930s, pp. 86-87; F-111 found unsuitable for carrier use in the 1960s, p. 92; work done at the Flight Test Division, Anacostia, in the mid-1930s, pp. 97-102, 105-107, 111, 167-169; new naval aircraft in the 1930s resulted from the combining of fleet requirements with BuAer expertise, pp. 103-104; operations of Navy flying boats in the late 1930s, pp. 112-116, discussion of role of aviation in the Navy in the 1930s, pp. 116-119; fitting out, commissioning, and early service of the USS Belleau Wood (CVL-24) in 1943-1944, pp. 122, 125-134; Pride's command of all naval air stations in the Central Pacific in 1944-1945, pp. 134-136; air support of U.S. amphibious forces as the Pacific War wound down in 1945, pp. 136-138; operations of Carrier divisions Six and Four in the Atlantic and Mediterranean in 1946-1947, pp. 147-148, 153-161; work of the Bureau of Aeronautics from 1947 to 1951, pp. 161-162, 171-189, 193-205; operations of Carrier Division Two in the Atlantic and Mediterranean in 1951-1952, pp. 205-209, 213-215; work of the Naval Air Test Center in the late 1940s and early 1950s, pp. 217-219; Pride's command of the Pacific Fleet Air Force, 1956-1959, pp. 231-233

Aviators
> See: Pilots; Landing Signal Officers

Baker Island
> Pacific island occupied by U.S. forces in September 1943, pp. 127-129

Battleships
> Used platforms on turret tops for launching aircraft in

the early post-World War I period, pp. 16-26, 162-166

Beachley, Lincoln
   Civilian stunt pilot who flew early in the 20th century, pp. 4-5

Belleau Wood USS (CVL-24)
   Pride's experiences as the first commanding officer of this light carrier in 1943-1944 during fitting out, commissioning, and early combat duty, pp. 122, 125-134

"Big Boy"
   See: Nuclear Weapons

Blimps
   Demise of lighter-than-air craft in the U.S. Navy in the 1950s, pp. 198-199

Bombing
   Development of dive-bombing by the Navy in the 1930s, pp. 86-88; by the U.S. Army Air Forces against Japan in World War II, pp. 140-142; potential for delivery of nuclear weapons by the Navy in the early 1950s, pp. 214-215, 217

Boston, Massachusetts
   Site of Pride's enlistment, training, and part of active naval service during World War I, pp. 7-10.

Brown, Charles R. ("Cat"), Rear Admiral, USN (USNA, 1921)
   Incident involving Brown and "Artie" Doyle while turning over command at Gibraltar in the early 1950s, pp. 209-210

BuAer
   See: Aeronautics, Bureau of

Bureaus--Naval
   See: Aeronautics; Naval Weapons; Navigation; Ordnance

Cabaniss, Robert W., Lieutenant Commander, USN (USNA, 1906)
   Strict disciplinarian as Navy flight instructor in 1917, p. 11

Carney, Robert B. ("Mick"), Admiral, USN (USNA, 1916)
   Chief of Naval Operations who picked Pride in 1953 to command the U.S. Seventh Fleet, p. 221

Carrier Division Two
   Operations in the Atlantic and Mediterranean in 1951-1952, pp. 205-209, 213-215

Carrier Pigeons
   Used to take messages ashore from aircraft carriers in the 1920s, pp. 55-58

Catapults
> Use of steam catapults in the 1950s made a vast improvement in carrier operations, p. 209

Central Intelligence Agency
> Director Allen Dulles asked Pride to get from the Taiwanese raw intelligence data on the Chinese Communists in the mid-1950s, pp. 230-231

Chase, Nathan B., Lieutenant Commander, USN (USNA 1912)
> Navy pilot who learned to fly land planes soon after the end of World War I, p. 163

Chatham, Massachusetts
> Site of Pride's post-World War I flying, including recruiting duty which resulted in the crash of an H-boat into the Connecticut River in 1919, pp. 163, 169-171

Chevalier, Godfrey deC., Lieutenant Commander, USN (USNA, 1910)
> Head of Atlantic Fleet Ship Plane Division circa 1920, pp. 17, 19; instructed Pride to develop carrier arresting gear in the 1920s, pp. 27, 33; made first carrier landing in 1922, p. 37

Chiang Kai-shek
> Nationalist Chinese President who had dealings with the U.S. Seventh Fleet in the mid-1950s, pp. 215, 227, 230-231

Chinese Communists
> Disruption of U.S. communications during a Seventh Fleet exercise in the mid-1950s, pp. 216-217; harassment of offshore islands in the 1950s, pp. 224, 228

Clark, Joseph J. ("Jocko"), Vice Admiral, USN (USNA, 1918)
> Had large staff on board flagship as Commander Seventh Fleet in 1952-1953, pp. 222-223

Coast Guard, U. S.
> Development of aircraft in tandem with the Navy in the late 1940s and early 1950s, pp. 203-204

Communications
> Demands placed on communications network during planning stages of Japanese invasion towards the end of World War II, pp. 141-142; delays in communications in the mid-1950s required the U.S. Seventh Fleet Commander to make decisions and take actions on his own, pp. 224, 226
>
> See also: Radio

Congress, U.S.
> Testimony to by the Chief of the Bureau of Aeronautics in the late 1940s and early 1950s, pp. 171-173; testimony by the Secretary of the Navy in the 1950s, p. 179; lack of influence on the awarding of aviation procurement contracts circa 1950, pp. 188-189

Contracts
> Reuben Fleet as Army Air Corps contracting officer after World War I, p. 191; contracts between BuAer and aircraft manufacturers in the 1940s and 1950s, pp. 187-189

Crete
> During visit in the late 1940s, Pride saw the remains of the British cruiser York which had been torpedoed at Suda Bay in 1941, p. 157

Cuba
> See: Guantanamo Bay, Cuba

Dayton, John H., Captain, USN (USNA, 1890)
> As commanding officer of the battleship Arizona (BB-39) in 1920, he didn't believe in the use of airplanes on ships, p. 23

Development--Aviation
> Experimentation with various types of carrier flight deck arresting gear in the 1920s, pp. 27-36, 43-44, 51-53, 73-74; development of aircraft carriers by foreign navies in the 1920s, pp. 67-69; naval aviation development work at the Experimental Division at Hampton Roads in the late 1920s and early 1930s, pp. 75-76, 79-85, 89-91; Army-Navy aircraft engine work in the 1930s, p. 94; testing of new aircraft by the Flight Test Section at Anacostia in the mid-1930s, pp. 97-102, 105-107, 111; BuAer engineers drew up specifications to develop new Navy aircraft in the 1930s, pp. 103-104, 108-110; development of guided missiles by the Navy in the late 1940s and early 1950s, pp. 173-174, 176-178; work on drones in the 1940s, pp. 174-176; progress on jet aircraft in the late 1940s and early 1950s, pp. 181-183; aircraft carrier angled decks, p. 197

Discipline
> Few disciplinary problems occurred among U.S. Sixth and Seventh Fleet sailors in the 1940s and 1950s, p. 159

Dive-bombers
> Tested by the Navy in the 1930s, pp. 85-88

Doyle, Austin K. ("Artie"), Rear Admiral, USN (USNA, 1920)
> Incident involving Doyle and "Cat" Brown while turning over command at Gibraltar in the early 1950s, pp. 209-210

Drones
    Development work by Captain D. S. Fahrney in the 1940s, pp. 174-176

Dulles, Allen
    Central Intelligence Agency director who asked Pride to have the Taiwanese submit raw intelligence data on the Chinese Communists in the mid-1950s, pp. 230-231

Education
    Pride's experiences around the time of World War I and before, pp. 1-4, 6, 8; Pride's postgraduate education in aeronautical engineering in the mid-1020s, pp. 46-47, 50-51

Eldorado, USS (AGC-11)
    Flagship of Vice Admiral Kelly Turner during the Okinawa operation in 1945, p. 137

Engineering Plants--Shipboard
    Diesel engines omitted from the USS Lexington (CV-2) and Saratoga (CV-3) when built in the 1920s, pp. 71-72; problems with salt in the condensers on board the light carrier Belleau Wood (CVL-24) in 1943, pp. 131-133

Experimental Division, Hampton Roads, Virginia
    Conducted naval aviation development work in the late 1920s and early 1930s, pp. 75-76, 79-85, 89-91

Fahrney, Delmer S., Captain, USN (USNA, 1920)
    Did development work on drones in the 1940s for which Pride would not recommend a decoration, pp. 174-175

Fighter Planes
    F4B-4 was the Navy's best fighter in the early 1930s, pp. 86, 91; F-111 controversy of the 1960s, p. 92; role of the Bureau of Aeronautics fighter desk in themid-1930s, pp. 108-112; reluctance of the Marine Corps to switch from propeller planes to jets in the late 1940s, pp. 181-182

Fighting Squadron Three (VF-3)
    Operations while under the command of Pride and Lieutenant Commander Miles Browning in the 1930s, pp. 86-89

Fitness Reports
    Pride got promotion help from Marc Mitscher after being held back by an "unsatisfactory" fitness report in the late 1930s, pp. 234-235

Fleet, Reuben
    Army Air Corps officer who founded Consolidated Aircraft Corporation in 1923 and had a long association with the Navy, pp. 191-193

Flight Test Section
    Experimental testing of aircraft done at Anacostia Naval Air Station in the mid-1930s, pp. 97-107, 111, 167-169

Florida
    See: Miami, Pensacola

Flying Boats
    Used by the U.S. Navy from the World War I era onward in various roles, pp. 12-16, 77-78; Patrol Wing One based on the tender Wright (AV-1) in the late 1930s, pp. 112-117; Pride crashed an H-boat in the Connecticut River in 1919, pp. 169-171

Foreign Navies
    Development of aircraft carriers in the 1920s, pp. 67-69

    See also: Japanese Navy, Royal Navy

Formosa
    See: Taiwan

Forrestal, James V.
    Concerns while serving as Secretary of the Navy in 1947, p. 180

Franke, William B.
    As Secretary of the Navy in 1959, he created the Bureau of Naval Weapons because of disagreements between BuAer and BuOrd over the control of guided missiles, pp. 178-179

French Army
    Night flying operations in World War I, pp. 79-80

G Forces
    Effect of during naval aircraft operations during the 1930s, pp. 87-88, 90-91

General Board of the U. S. Navy
    Deliberations concerning aircraft carrier tonnage in 1920s, pp. 69-71

Griffin, Virgil C. ("Squash"), Lieutenant Commander, USN (USNA, 1912)
    Made first carrier takeoff from the USS Langley (CV-1) in 1922, p. 37; involvement with the Langley's carrier pigeons, p. 56

Grumman, Roy F.
    Aircraft manufacturer who had a long association with Pride and the Navy, p. 190

Guantanamo Bay, Cuba
    Site of U.S. Navy training operations in the years just after World War I, pp. 20, 22, 25-26

Guided Missiles
    Development by the Navy in the late 1940s and early 1950s, pp. 172-174, 176-178; turf fight over whether missiles belong to the Bureau of Ordnance of the Bureau of Aeronautics, pp. 178-179

Hampton Roads
    See: Norfolk, Virginia

Harris, Field, Major General, USMC (USNA, 1917)
    Reluctance about buying jet aircraft for the Marine Corps in the late 1940s, pp. 181-182

Hawaii
    See: Pearl Harbor

Heinemann, Edward H.
    Topflight designer for Douglas Aircraft Corporation for many years, pp. 195-196

Helicopters
    Development work involving the Bureau of Aeronautics in the late 1940s, pp. 199-203

    See also: Autogiro

Howland Island
    Pacific Island occupied by U.S. forces in September 1943, pp. 127-129

Italy
    Visits to by U.S. Sixth Fleet ships in the late 1940s, pp. 156-159

Japan
> Plans for U.S. invasion of at the end of World War II, pp. 138-141; U.S. bombing of in 1945, pp. 140-143; reaction of Nagasaki mayor to American visit in the mid-1950s, p. 144; possibility of trickery at the time of surrender in 1945, p. 146; relationship with the U.S. Seventh Fleet in the mid-1950s, p. 229

Japanese Navy
> Development of aircraft carriers in the 1920s, p. 69; torpedoing of the USS Saratoga (CV-3) in early 1942, pp. 123-124; kamikaze attacks on the carrier Belleau Wood (CVL-24) in 1944, pp. 129-130, 133-134

Jet Aircraft
> Development of by the Navy's Bureau of Aeronautics in the late 1940s and early 1950s, pp. 181-183; in 1947, Pride was the first Navy flag officer to fly a jet, pp. 219-220

Kagoshima, Japan
> Description of terrain which would have made a U.S. landing difficult in World War II, pp. 139-140

Kaman, Charles H.
> Helicopter manufacturer who got support from the Navy's Bureau of Aeronautics around 1950, pp. 200-202

Kamikazes
> Attacks by Japanese suicide planes on the light carrier Belleau Wood (CVL-24) in 1944, pp. 129-130, 133-134

Korean War
> Impact on the Navy's Bureau of aeronautics, pp. 184-185; did not have much effect on Sixth Fleet operations in the early 1950s, pp. 213-214; Commander Seventh Fleet carried a large staff on board his flagship during the war, pp. 222-223

Land, Emory S., Captain, CC USN (USNA, 1902)
> BuAer officer who helped Pride get into postgraduate school in the mid-1920s, pp. 45-46

Landing Signal Officers
> Development of LSO concept by Commander Kenneth Whiting in early 1920s, pp. 61-63

Langley, USS (CV-1)
    The U.S. Navy's first aircraft carrier, which served as an early test platform for sea-based aviation in the 1920s, pp. 27-37; operations following commissioning in 1922, pp. 39-44, 53, 56-57, 61-63, 68, 88-89; test of autogiro on board in 1931, pp. 84-85

LeMay, Curtis E., Major General, USA
    Army Air Forces officer who was involved in the dropping of atomic bombs on Japan in 1945, pp. 140-141

Lexington, USS (CV-2)
    Aircraft carrier commissioned in 1927 for fleet service, pp. 31, 35-36, 44-45, 51-55, 57-61, 63-70, 73-74

Logistics
    Allocation of scarce resources to naval air bases in the Pacific in World War II, pp. 134-135

LSO
    See: Landing Signal Officers

Maintenance
    Navy pilots assisted in work on their aircraft in the era following World War I, p. 26; maintenance suffered in the Navy in the 1950s as a result of the demands of the Korean War, p. 185

Marine Corps
    Reluctance about buying jet aircraft in the late 1940s, pp. 181-182

Marshall, Albert W., Captain, USN (USNA, 1896)
    First commanding officer of the carrier Lexington (CV-2), he arranged for flight operations in 1928 before those of the USS Saratoga (CV-3), p. 64

Massachusetts
    See: Boston, Chatham

Massachusetts Institute of Technology (MIT)
    Site of naval training during World War I, pp. 7, 11; Pride received postgraduate education in aeronautical engineering at MIT in the mid-1920s, pp. 46-47

Material, Office of Naval
    Established in the Navy Department right after World War II, pp. 144-145

McDonnell, James S.
    Founder of McDonnell Aircraft Corporation and someone who had a long association with the Navy, pp. 193-194

Medicine
　　Commander Morton D. Willcutts, MC, used a new surgical procedure in 1934 to save Pride's damaged leg rather than amputating it, pp. 167-168

Mediterranean Sea
　　Operations of Carrier Divisions Six and Four in the Mediterranean in 1946-1947, pp. 147-149, 151-161; operations of Carrier Division Two in 1951-1952, pp. 206-210, 213-215, 217

Megee, Vernon E., Colonel, USMC
　　Chief of staff to Pride during the Okinawa operation in 1945, p. 138

Miami, Florida
　　Site of Navy flight training in World War I, pp. 12-14

Midway (CVB-41) Class
　　Aircraft carriers which operated in the Sixth Fleet in the early 1950s, even though the Korean War was in progress, p. 214

Missiles
　　See: Guided Missiles

MIT
　　See: Massachusetts Institute of Technology

Mitscher, Marc A., Captain, USN (USNA, 1910)
　　Made first takeoff and landing on the USS Saratoga (CV-3) in 1928, p. 64; duty with Patrol Wing One in the late 1930s, pp. 113, 115, 233-235

Moffett, William A., Rear Admiral, USN (USNA, 1890)
　　First Chief of the Bureau of Aeronautics was a great friend naval aviation in the 1920s and 1930s, p. 118

Mullinnix, Henry M., Commander, USN (USNA, 1916)
　　Executive officer of the seaplane tender Wright (AV-1) who inadvertently wrote an "unsatisfactory" fitness report on Pride in the late 1930s, pp. 234-235

Nagasaki, Japan
　　Lack of animosity on the part of Japanese toward Americans there in the mid-1950s, p. 144

NATO
　　See: North Atlantic Treaty Organization

Naval Air Test Center, Patuxent River, Maryland
　　Testing of new naval aircraft in the late 1940 and early 1950s, pp. 217-219

Naval Aviation
　　See: Aviation--Naval

Naval Aviators
　　See: Pilots; Landing Signal Officers

Naval Disarmament Treaties
　　See: Disarmament Treaties--Naval

Naval Postgraduate School, Annapolis
　　Site of preliminary course in the mid-1920s before students went on to civilian universities, pp. 46-47, 50-51

Naval Reserve
　　Pride's service in the reserve from 1917 to 1921 before he became a regular officer, pp. 6-26; Pride transferred from the reserve to the regular Navy in 1921, pp. 48-49

Naval Weapons, Bureau of
　　See: Weapons, Bureau of Naval

Navigation, Bureau of
　　Delayed sending commission as commander to Pride in the late 1930s because of an "unsatisfactory" fitness report, pp. 234-235

Netherlands Navy
　　Participation in NATO exercises in the Mediterranean in the early 1950s, p. 207

Night Flying Operations
　　From U. S. aircraft carriers in the 1920s, p. 61; development of carrier deck lighting systems in the late 1920s, pp. 79-80

Noble, Albert C., Rear Admiral, USN (USNA, 1917)
　　As Chief of the Bureau of Ordnance in the late 1940s, he claimed cognizance over the Navy's guided missile development work, pp. 178-179

Norden, Carl L.
　　Civilian consultant who worked for the Navy in the 1920s on aircraft carrier arresting gear, pp. 35, 51-52, 74

Norfolk, Virginia
　　Carrier pigeons from the USS Langley (CV-1) returned to roost at the Norfolk Navy Yard in the early 1920s after being released at sea, pp. 55-57; site of aviation development work in the Experimental Division, Hampton Roads, in the late 1920s, pp. 75-76, 79-85, 89-90; recruiters for civilian companies set up shop outside the gate of the Navy base in the late 1940s, p. 160

North Atlantic Treaty Organization (NATO)
　　International operations between U.S. and allied naval vessels in the Mediterranean in the early 1950s, pp. 207-208

Nuclear Weapons
　　Use of atomic bombs against Japan in 1945, pp. 140-144; storage of nuclear devices on board Sixth Fleet aircraft carriers for possible use in the early 1950s, pp. 214-215, 217

O3U-6 (Corsair)
　　Pride had a spectacular crash in an XO3U-6 pontoon plane in 1934, pp. 97-99, 167-169

Okinawa
　　Air support of the U.S. amphibious forces taking part in the conquest of this Pacific island in 1945, pp. 136-137

Ordnance, Bureau of
　　Navy material bureau which was merged with the Bureau of Aeronautics in 1959 to form the Bureau of Naval Weapons, pp. 176-178

Panama Canal
　　Lamp posts next to the canal locks were knocked over when the carrier Lexington (CV-2) went through for the first time in 1928, pp. 65-66

Patrol Wing One
　　Collection of seaplane squadrons which operated from the tender Wright (AV-1) in the late 1930, pp. 112-116, 233-235

Patuxent River, Maryland
　　See: Naval Air Test Center

Pearl Harbor, Oahu, Hawaii
    Carrier Saratoga (CV-3) arrived at Pearl following the Japanese attack in 1941, pp. 71-72, 123; headquarters for Pride when he commanded naval air stations in the Central Pacific area in 1944-1945, pp. 134-136

Pensacola, Florida
    Site of Navy flight training in World War I, pp. 14-15.

Piasecki, Frank
    Helicopter developer who supplied a number of aircraft to the Navy, p. 202

Pigeons
    See: Carrier Pigeons

Pilots
    Early operations from the carrier Langley (CV-1) in the 1920s, pp. 37, 61-63; in the Lexington (CV-2) and Saratoga (CV-3) in the late 1920s, p. 64; ability to fly both carrier planes and land-based patrol planes, pp. 77-78; effect on pilots of G forces during dive-bombing in the 1930s, pp. 87-88; Japanese kamikaze attacks on the light carrier Belleau Wood (CVL-24) in 1944, pp. 129-130, 132-133

    See also Aviation--Civilian

Planning
    Plans concerning possible landings against China and Japan at the end of World War II, pp. 137-141; U.S. Seventh Fleet plans to react to possible Chinese Communist or Soviet actions in the mid-1950s, pp. 228-229

Point Mugu, California
    Development of Pacific missile testing range by the Navy in the late 1940s, pp. 172-174

Pride, Alfred Melville ("Mel"), Admiral, USN (Ret.)
    Education prior to entering the Navy, pp. 1-4, 6, 8; family of, pp. 1-2, 6-7, 106-107; Navy experiences during the World War I period, pp. 7-16, 77; member of Atlantic Fleet Ship Plane Division shortly after World War I, pp. 17-26, 163-166; development of flight deck arresting gear while in the crew of the USS Langley (CV-1) in the early 1920s, pp. 27-36; the Langley's operations while Pride was a member of the crew in the early 1920s, pp. 37, 39-45, 53, 56-57, 61-63;

postgraduate education at Annapolis and MIT in the mid-1920s, pp. 46-47, 50-51; transfer from the reserve to the regular Navy in 1921, pp. 48-49; service in the USS Lexington (CV-2) when she was fitting out and first went into service in 1927, pp. 51-55, 57-61, 63-68, 72-74; as executive officer of the carrier Saratoga (CV-3) in 1941 and at the beginning of World War II, pp. 71-72, 120-124; aviation development work at the experimental division at Hampton Roads in the late 1920s and early 1930s, pp. 74-76, 79-85, 89-91; command of Fighting Squadron three in the early 1930s, pp. 86-89; as Navy working member of the Aeronautical Board in the 1930s, pp. 92-96; command of the Flight Test Division, Anacostia, in the mid-1930s, pp. 97-107, 167-169; duty on the fighter desk in the Bureau of Aeronautics in the mid-1930s, pp. 108-112; as air officer and Patrol Wing One staff officer on board the seaplane tender Wright (AV-1) in the late 1930s, pp. 112-117, 233-235; as commanding officer of the light carrier Belleau Wood (CVL-24) in 1943-1944, pp. 122, 125-134; command of all naval air stations in the Central Pacific in 1944-1945, pp. 134-136; command of air support units for U.S. Amphibious Forces Pacific in 1945, pp. 136-144; duty in the Office of Naval Material right after World War II pp. 144-145; as Commander Carrier Divisions Six and Four in 1946-1947, pp. 147-149, 151-61; duty as Chief of the Bureau of Aeronautics from 1947-1951, pp. 161-162, 171-178, 180-189, 193-205; as the first Navy flag officer to fly a jet aircraft, pp. 219-220; as Commander Carrier Division Two in the Atlantic and Mediterranean in 1951-1952, pp. 205-209, 213-215; command of the Naval Air Test Center, Patuxent River, Maryland in 1951-1953, pp. 217-219; command of the Seventh Fleet from 1953 to 1955, pp. 144, 215-217, 221-231 as Commander Air Force Pacific Fleet from 1956 to 1959, pp. 231-233

Radar
Projected to be of little use in planned invasion of Japan towards the end of World War II, p. 140

Radio
Use of by naval aircraft to spot ships' gunfire in the 1920s, pp. 58-59; Red Chinese blanked out communications of the U.S. Seventh Fleet in the mid-1950s, pp. 215-216

Reenlistments
Difficulty keeping men in the Navy right after World War II, pp. 160-161

Research and Development
See: Development--Aviation

Rochester, USS (CA-124)
    Became flagship of the U.S. Seventh Fleet in early 1954 when the size of the fleet commander's staff was reduced, pp. 222-223

Rosendahl, Charles E., Vice Admiral, USN (Ret.) (USNA, 1914)
    Lighter-than-air advocate who was unhappy with lack of support from Pride in the late 1940s, p. 198

Royal Navy
    Aircraft carrier arresting gear used in the early 1920s, pp. 29-32, 73; intelligence collection about the USS Langley (CV-1) in the 1920s, p. 68; British cruiser York sunk by Italian torpedoes at Suda Bay, Crete, in 1941, p. 157; development of aircraft carrier angled deck in the 1950s, p. 197

Saratoga, USS (CV-3)
    Aircraft carrier commissioned in 1927 for fleet service, pp. 31, 36, 44-45, 57-60, 63-64, 66, 68-71; operations in 1941 and 1942, pp. 71-72, 120-124

Seaplanes
    See: Flying Boats

Secretary of Defense
    Now makes decisions which used to be settled at a much lower level in the military services, p. 188

Secretary of the Navy
    Relationship with the Chief of the Bureau of Aeronautics in the 1940s and 1950s, pp. 171, 178-180

Seventh Fleet, U.S.
    Operations in the Western Pacific between 1953 and 1955, pp. 144, 159, 215-216, 221-229; size of the staff cut in half when the fleet commander moved to a cruiser as flagship in 1954, pp. 222-223

Ship Design
    Decisions concerning the tonnage of the aircraft carriers Lexington (CV-2) and Saratoga (CV-3) in the 1920s, pp. 69-71; carrier deck lighting experiments in the late 1920s, pp. 79-80

    See Also: Arresting Gear

Shiphandling
: Pride's experiences as commanding officer of the carrier Belleau Wood (CVL-24) in 1943-1944, pp. 122, 130, 132; comparison of characteristics of various carrier classes, pp. 151-152; Pride's experiences in battleships circa 1920, p. 164

Sikorsky, Igor
: Helicopter developer who supplied a number of aircraft to the Navy over the years, pp. 199, 202

Sixth Fleet
: Deployment to the Mediterranean of Carrier Divisions Six and Four in 1946-1947, pp. 147-149, 151-161; deployment to of Carrier Division Two in 1951-1952, pp. 206-210, 213-215, 217

Soviet Union
: Trustworthiness of Soviets doubted by some U.S. officials towards the end of World War II, p. 147; U.S. concern over possible Soviet actions in Asia in the mid-1950s, pp. 214, 228-229

Specifications
: Standardized in the 1930s for aircraft and aviation equipment by the U.S. Aeronautical Board, pp. 93-96; drawn up for Navy planes in the 1930s by the Bureau of Aeronautics, pp. 103-104, 108-110

Spotting of Naval Gunfire
: See: Atlantic Fleet Ship Plane Division

State Department
: Role in licensing aviation equipment for foreign sales in the 1930s, p. 95; concern with Seventh Fleet operations in the mid-1950s, p. 230

Stevens, Leslie C., Lieutenant Commander, CC, USN (USNA, 1919)
: Naval constructor who suggested elimination of fore-and-aft arresting wires on aircraft carrier decks in the late 1920s, pp. 31, 73

Stump, Felix B., Admiral, USN (USNA, 1917)
: As Commander in Chief, U.S. Pacific Fleet, in the mid 1950s, he supported the work of Pride as Commander Seventh Fleet, p. 224

Surgery
  Commander Morton D. Willcutts, MC, used a new surgical procedure in 1934 to save Pride's damaged leg rather than amputating it, pp. 167-168

Tachen Islands
  Islands off the mainland of China which were evacuated in the mid-1950s because of Chinese Communist actions, pp. 224-226

Taiwan
  Relationship of the people and government with the U.S. Seventh Fleet in the mid-1950s, pp. 215, 224-228, 230-231

Tate, Jackson R., Ensign, USN
  A naval officer who became an aviator in the 1920s and had a peculiar faculty for telling the truth and making it sound like a lie, pp. 211-212

Testing of Aircraft
  See: Experimental Division; Flight Test Section; Naval Air Test Center

Test Pilots
  See: Flight Test Section

Texas, USS (BB-35)
  Used in 1919 to test program of flying spotting planes from battleship turrets, pp. 19-20

Torpedoes
  Damaged the USS Saratoga (CV-3) in an early 1942 attack, pp. 123-124; sank the British cruiser York at Suda Bay, Crete, in 1941, p. 157

Training
  Pride's initial indoctrination in the Navy in 1917, followed by aviation training in Massachusetts and Florida, pp. 7-8, 11-15; Navy pilots trained with the Army Air Corps in 1919 to fly land planes, pp. 17-18

Treaties
  See: Disarmament Treaties--Naval

Turkey
  Visits to by U.S. Sixth Fleet ships in the late 1940s, pp. 155-156.

Wright, USS (AV-1)
    Seaplane tender which served the flying boats of Patrol Wing One in the late 1930s, pp. 112-116, 233-235

XO3U-6
    See: O3U-6 (Corsair)

York, HMS
    British cruiser sunk by Italian torpedoes at Suda Bay, Crete, in 1941, p. 157

www.ingramcontent.com/pod-product-compliance
Lightning Source LLC
Chambersburg PA
CBHW080615170426
43209CB00007B/1437